Love in London

Studies in Austrian Literature, Culture, and Thought

Translation Series

Theodor Kramer

LOVE IN LONDON

Translated by
Frederick Brainin
and
Jörg Thunecke

With an Afterword by
Jörg Thunecke

ARIADNE PRESS

Ariadne Press would like to express its appreciation to the Austrian Cultural Institute, New York, and the Theodor Kramer Gesellschaft, Vienna, for assistance in publishing this book.

Dual language edition based on Theodor Kramer, *Gesammelte Gedichte*, 3 vols., ©1984-1987 Europa Verlag, Vienna.

Library of Congress Cataloging-in-Publication Data

Kramer, Theodor.
    Love in London / Theodor Kramer ; translated by Frederick Brainin and Jörg Thunecke ; afterword by Jörg Thunecke.
        p.   cm. -- (Studies in Austrian literature, culture, and thought. Translation series)
    ISBN 1-57241-009-4
    I. Brainin, Frederick, 1913-   . II. Thunecke, Jörg. III. Title.
IV. Series.
PT2621.R19A23   1995
831'.912--dc20
                                        94-29276
                                        CIP

Cover design:
Willy Pechtel

CONTENTS

W.P.92

2

THE OLD ACCORDIONIST

3

NICHT FÜRS SÜSSE, NUR FÜRS SCHARFE . . .

Nicht fürs Süße, nur fürs Scharfe
und fürs Bittre bin ich da;
schlag, ihr Leute, nicht die Harfe,
spiel die Ziehharmonika.

Leer, verfilzt ist meine Tasche
und durchlöchert ist mein Hut;
daß ich leb, das Herz aus Asche,
macht: aus Branntwein ist mein Blut.

Ließ das Salz der Tränen Spuren,
wären meine Gucker blind;
meine Liebsten sind die Huren,
mir Gesellen Staub und Wind.

Das Falsett, das möcht umarmen,
doch das Ganze trägt der Baß;
hab Erbarmen, brauch Erbarmen,
doch zuinnerst haust der Haß.

Weiß zuviel und möcht doch träumen
wie der Echs im Sonnenschein;
leeres Brausen in den Bäumen,
braus für mich, nick träg ich ein!

Darf nicht ruhn, muß Straßen weiter;
denn bald bin ich nicht mehr da,
und es spielt die Stadt kein Zweiter
so die Ziehharmonika.

THE OLD ACCORDIONIST

Not for what's sweet but for what's sharp
and for what's bitter have I come;
people, do not pluck the harp,
strike up the old accordion.

My bag is empty but for suint,
and my hat is full of gaps;
I am alive (my heart's ashed print!)
because my blood does burn like *Schnaps*.

If all my tears leave salty traces
my eyes they surely would go blind;
my lovers are whores best for embraces,
my fellows are the dust and wind.

Falsetto only love itself,
but bass with all men wants to mate;
have pity, o, do pity yourself,
when eating your guts there still is hate.

Know life's truth well, yet want to dream
like lizards on a sun-baked bluff;
the storm in trees at sundown's gleam
does roar for me while I doze off!

Can't take a rest, must move on, brother,
for in time soon I'll be gone,
and on the town shall play no other
like I the old accordion.

6

PART I

THE LAST DAYS IN VIENNA (1938)

AN EINE JUNGE FREUNDIN

Sacht schließen hinter uns die Türen;
laß bis zum Eck mit dir mich gehn
und an den Mund die Hand mich führen . . .
wir werden uns nicht wiedersehn.
Es ist nicht nur, weil oft zu rasten
mir ziemt, weil meine Börse leer;
damit würd ich dich noch belasten,
doch was uns trennt, ist etwas mehr.

Für dich mit deinen zwanzig Jahren
ist alles klar und nichts verzwickt;
ich aber bin zutiefst zerfahren,
hellhörig leb ich, eingedickt
sind meine Säfte um die Flachsen.
Mich quält noch viel, an dem du, Kind,
vorbei schon lebst; du bist erwachsen,
ich bin schon alt und doch ein Kind.

Mit deinem festen Mund, zum Pfeifen
geschaffen, praktisch und gescheit,
wirst du mich nie so recht begreifen;
in mir geht eine ganze Zeit,
zu weit gespannt und schwer, zu Ende.
So scharf und viel wie ich zu sehn,
hast du nicht nötig; deine Hände
sind gut . . . du wirst mich nicht mehr sehn.

TO A YOUNG GIRLFRIEND

The doors behind us softly close;
lets walk to the corner together, and then
I'll lift your hand to my mouth in repose . . .
I know that we won't meet again.
It's not because from love an old cat
should often take breaks–my money's spent;
I'd gladly burden you with that,
but what parts us is more than the rent.

For you of twenty-or-so-years
all's clear and free of narrow sluices;
but to my core I'm seized with fear,
too keen of sounds, my body juices
around the tendons feeling clotty.
Still hurt by things that away you've filed,
you grown-up woman in soul and body,
I feel I'm old and yet a child.

With a firm mouth you're whistling tunes
so cheerfully that I put them to rhyme,
you've never felt the deep-seated wounds,
when forced into exile before your time.
A visionary misunderstood
let me be; I know that when
I kiss your calloused hands they're good . . .
We'll part and never meet again.

DIE WAHRHEIT IST, MAN HAT
MIR NICHTS GETAN

Die Wahrheit ist, man hat mir nichts getan.
Ich darf schon lang in keiner Zeitung schreiben,
die Mutter darf noch in der Wohnung bleiben.
Die Wahrhheit ist, man hat mir nichts getan.

Der Greisler schneidet mir den Schinken an
und dankt mir, wenn ich ihn bezahle, kindlich;
wovon ich leben werd, ist unerfindlich.
Die Wahrheit ist, man hat mir nichts getan.

Ich fahr wie früher mit der Straßenbahn
und gehe unbehelligt durch die Gassen;
ich weiß bloß nicht, ob sie mich gehen lassen.
Die Wahrheit ist, man hat mir nichts getan.

Es öffnet sich mir in kein Land die Bahn,
ich kann mich nicht von selbst von hinnen heben:
ich habe einfach keinen Raum zum Leben.
Die Wahrheit ist, man hat mir nichts getan.

THE TRUTH IS NOT A THING
THEY'VE DONE TO ME

The truth is not a thing they've done to me.
For many months no paper's run my poem.
My mother's still allowed to keep her home.
The truth is, not a thing they've done to me.

The grocer slices me the ham, solicitously
he thanks me for my cash-paid patronage;
how shall I make a living, just for my ménage?
The truth is not a thing they've done to me.

I ride the tramcars as before, I'm free
to walk the streets, where no soul ever caused me grief;
but will they let me go, clean air again to sniff?
The truth is not a thing they've done to me.

No railroad track has switched for me to flee,
I can't depart by air all by myself:
I've simply got no space in which to delve.

The truth is not a thing they've done to me.

AN MEIN KAFFEEHAUS

Wo schwere Wagen fahren
vorüber in der Näh,
beim Zollamt, steht seit Jahren
mein kleines Volkscafé.
Das Glas ist abgeschlagen,
in ihre Fugen fliehn
die Asseln; schon seit Tagen
geh ich nun nicht mehr hin.

Sacht tropft die Wasserleitung,
es stützt sich gut aufs Kinn;
ein andrer liest die Zeitung,
es steht auch wenig drin.
Ich war, wenn dort die Wände
mich bargen, erst zu Haus;
dort schrieb ich viele Bände,
damit ist es nun aus.

Ich mach mir keine Zeichen,
längst bleibt mein Merkheft leer;
ein Mensch wie meinesgleichen
hat nichts zu schreiben mehr.
Er braucht auch nicht zu lesen,
es gilt nicht, was er tut;
kaum kehrt wie Staub der Besen
ihn fort mit schwarzem Sud.

TO MY CAFÉ

Where heavy trucks pass near
the customs night and day,
there open, for many a year,
I've found my little café.
The glass is cracked in places,
for wood-lice rain-safe haunts;
for days now its boxed spaces
for me are out of bounds.

Where slowly drips the pipe,
you're propping up your chin;
someone reads a tabloid's gripe,
forgetting the world's din.
There (sheltered by thick walls!)
I only felt at home;
many notebooks I filled in its stalls,
that's gone now like beer's foam.

No single new impression
my diary's noted for weeks;
a man like me under depression
the snow of white pages seeks.
No sense to read books either, who
cares what poet I quote;
the dust pan with the black brew
shall sweep me out like a mote.

Jetzt schlägt es draußen sieben,
ich will bald schlafen gehn;
von dem, was ich geschrieben,
bleibt dies und das wohl stehn.
Wenn zwei sich's weitergeben
bei einer Schale Tee,
dann sitz ich still daneben
im himmlischen Café.

Outside the clock strikes seven,
soon sleep shall ease my pain;
of what my pen's engraving
this and that shall remain.
When lovers (my verse recites them!)
meet over tea some day,
then I sit still beside them
at the heavenly café.

VON DER ANGST

So gewaltig ist nichts und nichts läßt so nicht ruhn,
wie die Angst, die den Menschen befällt,
wenn es ihm nicht erlaubt ist, sein Tagwerk zu tun
und er gar nichts mehr gilt auf der Welt.
Wie ein Schlafwandler, der jäh erwacht aus dem Traum
auf dem First, steht er da und nichts bietet im Raum
seinem Griff sich, woran er sich hält.

Er sieht niemanden an und betritt keinen Schank,
denn er meint, ihm ist mehr noch verwehrt,
als man ihm schon verwehrte; das macht ihn so krank,
daß er selber sich alles erschwert.
Er verbrennt seine Bücher und Schriften, ihm fällt
auch die Feder, wie krampfhaft er immer sie hält,
in die Glut, weil die Angst an ihm zehrt.

Seinen Reis trägt er früh unterm Mantel scheu heim;
eh gekündigt wird, räumt er das Haus.
Was die Welt von ihm weiß, hält er ängstlich geheim,
und das Heimlichste plaudert er aus.
Wo er niedersitzt, schweigt er und macht sich ganz klein,
und er scharrte am liebsten für immer sich ein
vor der Zeit, wie im Winkel die Maus.

Und ein kleines, so ist er zu nichts mehr imstand,
nicht zu fahrn mit der Bahn noch zu gehn;
ihm verschwimmt, was er sieht, ihm gehorcht nicht die
            Hand,
doch er kann nicht von selber vergehn,
ob das Lied ihm auch zuckt, ob der Schlaf ihn auch
            flieht;
und er stöhnt, wenn ihn nachts niemand hört oder sieht:
Laßt es bald, laßt es heut noch geschehn!

OF MAN'S GREATEST FEAR

There's nothing more shocking, incessantly felt,
than the fear, which befalls a man,
when he is sacked from the job he's held,
and he never matters again.
Like a sleepwalker waking up from his dream
on roof's ridge he stands there unable to scream,
holding on to a bottomless plan.

He looks at no one and enters no bar,
for he thinks there's more to his ban
from public park bench and tramway car,
what makes him feel less than a man.
He burns his books and scripts, and his pen
(as tightly as he may uphold his ken!)
for fear feeds on him, smiling wan.

His rice he carries home with him hidden
under his coat; he moves out
before he's evicted. Anxiety ridden
a secret he keeps what about
him is known, yet talks to the mob;
wherever he rests he'd rather sob
in his sleep: a rat in a rout.

And only too soon he stops functioning,
walking or taking a train;
his eyesight blurred, his hand a strange thing,
yet to plan his own death is in vain
(with his eyelid's twitch, his insomnia's tease!)
and he moans, when at night him no soul hears or sees:
may soon come the dreaded black pain!

WER LÄUTET DRAUSSEN AN DER TÜR?

Wer läutet draußen an der Tür,
kaum daß es sich erhellt?
Ich geh schon, Schatz. Der Bub hat nur
die Semmeln hingestellt.

Wer läutet draußen an der Tür?
Bleib nur; ich geh, mein Kind.
Es war ein Mann, der fragte an
beim Nachbarn, wer wir sind.

Wer läutet draußen an der Tür?
Laß ruhig die Wanne voll.
Die Post war da; der Brief ist nicht
dabei, der kommen soll.

Wer läutet draußen an der Tür?
Leg du die Betten aus.
Der Hausbesorger war's; wir solln
am Ersten aus dem Haus.

Wer läutet draußen an der Tür?
Die Fuchsien blühn so nah.
Pack, Liebste, mir mein Waschzeug ein
und wein nicht: sie sind da.

WHO RINGS THE BELL OUTSIDE

Who rings the bell outside?–It tolls,
when dawn's still gray as slag.
I'll get it, love. Just Viennese rolls,
the boy's left in a bag.

Who rings the bell again?–Let it toll.
You stay, I'll see what's the fuss.
It was a man who neighbors did poll
on Jewish folks like us.

Who keeps on ringing the bell?–Some ruse?
Fill up the bathtub, please.
It was the mailman; but no news
we expect from friends overseas.

Our doorbell rings, who can be that?
You make up the beds for the day.
The janitor it was . . . our flat
to vacate on the first of May.

Who rings the front doorbell?–That's it.
The fuchsias bloom so near.
My dearest, pack my bathroom kit,
and do not cry: they're here.

WIEN, FRONLEICHNAM 1939

Wenige waren es, die Stellung nahmen
unterm Himmel, um zur Stadt zu gehn;
als sie singend ihres Weges kamen,
blieben viele auf den Steigen stehn.

Schütter quoll der Weihrauch und die Reiser
längs der Straße standen schier entlaubt;
klagend sang der kleine Chor sich heiser
und das Volk entblößte still das Haupt.

Manche kannten nur vom Hörensagen
noch den Umgang; doch dem baren Haar
tat es wohl, daß selbst in diesen Tagen
irgendetwas manchen heilig war.

Und indessen sie dem Zug nachstarrten,
salzigen Auges, Mannsvolk, Weib und Kind,
schwenkten aus den Fenstern die Standarten
alle das verbogne Kreuz im Wind.

CORPUS CHRISTI, VIENNA 1939

Few but assembled for the procession outdoor,
walking while singing to the Inner City;
after Whitsun, seven days plus four,
many, on sidewalks, begged God's pity.

Thin rose the incense, the broomlike trees coarse
along the street stood leafless, almost dead;
lamenting the small choir sang itself hoarse,
and silently the people bared their head.

From hearsay only some knew the chimes
announcing the passage . . . Yet with their bared hair
it felt so good that even in these times
there were some holy things with folks to share.

And while they salty-eyed stared after the march,
the menfolk, wives and children–bless God's *Kind*!–
there from the windows, blood-red on white starch,
the crooked cross waved in late May's wind.

DAS KONSULAT

Muß fort, ob ich es auch nicht mag
und ob ich auch nichts tat;
drum steh ich Schlange Tag für Tag
vorm fremden Konsulat.

Der Staub liegt im Logis schon dick,
der Koffer ist gepackt;
trotz dickem Rock vor jedem Blick
fühl ich mich splitternackt.

So stand ich oft schon da im Traum,
steh nicht zum letzten Mal;
das weiße Pulver selbst hilft kaum
mir aus der müden Qual.

Ein Schranken stand im trüben Licht,
da wurd das Aug mir naß;
hilf Gott, ich hätt das Visum nicht
in meinem Reisepaß.

THE CONSULATE

Must leave, though loath to go away,
and though no soul I hate:
that's why in queues I hug each day
the foreignconsulate.

The dust lies in my lodgings high,
I'm packed, in my strange mood
(despite my heavy overcoat!) I
feel like one in the nude.

That way I often stood adream,
will dream no doubt again;
not even the white powder's gleam
can kill my tired pain.

In twilight's mist a frontier gate
was raised, my eyes blurred damp . . .
God help me if no consulate
had given me my visa stamp.

PART II

THIS ISLAND CALLED HOME (1939)

VON DEN ERSTEN TAGEN IN LONDON

In London treib ich mich seit ein paar Tagen
herum, die Koffer stehn noch eingestellt;
wohin ich komm, hör ich die gleichen Fragen,
wie es mir Neuling hierzuland gefällt.
So groß die Stadt auch ist, sie dünkt mich ländlich
mit ihren Gassen, ganz von Grün verschönt;
im Hydepark liegt das Volk wie selbstverständlich:
ich aber bin daran noch nicht gewöhnt.

Mit Auskunft dient mir, wen ich frage, willig,
doch läßt er mich beileibe nicht heran;
es tut ihm leid, er hält es nicht für billig,
daß ich im eignen Land nicht schreiben kann.
Daß man zuweilen meinesgleichen endlich
die Straßen waschen läßt und ihn verhöhnt,
erscheint den Leuten vollends unverständlich:
ich aber bin daran schon längst gewöhnt.

Der Fisch ist billig, doch das Wohnen teuer,
die Butter salzig und das Wasser schal;
sind die Entfernungen auch ungeheuer,
nicht sitzen bleiben kann ich nach dem Mahl.
Daß man nicht immer lächelt, wenn man endlich
beherbergt wird, und aus dem Schlaf noch stöhnt,
dünkt hierzuland die Leute unverständlich:
ich aber bin noch nicht an sie gewöhnt.

THE FIRST DAYS IN LONDON

For days now I've been a tourist drifting through London
with my baggage put up at Victoria station;
wherever I go, folks ply me with abandon
how this newcomer likes his immigration.
The City's big but has a village source
with courtyards and street greens overdone a bit;
folks lie in Hyde Park as a matter of course:
but I still haven't gotten used to it.

Serving my inquiries each passer-by is,
yet keeps his distance from this bloke all right;
he's really sorry, taking it amiss
that in my country poems I cannot write.
That people of my kind they let in my land
wash streets and then run through a rain of spit
seems what the folks here'll never understand:
but long ago I've gotten used to it.

The fish is cheap, yet rents rise all around,
the butter's salty and the water's stale;
great distances here shrink by underground,
but I can't nurse in peace my post-lunch ale.
Night clerks ignore it when (late lodged at last!)
asleep you're moaning in a nightmarish fit . . .;
they think next wall two folks their love broadcast:
but I still haven't gotten used to it.

HANOVER SQUARE

Wir wohnen sechzehn Wochen schon
im kleinen Boardinghaus;
für uns schrillt nie das Telefon,
bald geht das Geld uns aus.
Stets rümpft die Nase das Gesind,
riechts es den Waschgeruch;
es flockt der Ruß, der Regen rinnt,
und langsam wächst das Buch.

Die alten Kragen tun es noch,
zwängt sie die Spange zu;
und Tinte deckt das böse Loch
in deinem Stöckelschuh.
Zum Trödler trägst du aus dem Spind
manch Stück im Fransentuch;
es flockt der Ruß, der Regen rinnt,
und langsam wächst das Buch.

Nur selten summt der Kessel zwar,
fast ist die Büchse leer;
kahl schaut, der grün beim Einziehn war,
herein der kleine Square.
Kaum kommt, wenn wir beim Nachtmahl sind,
die Katz noch zu Besuch;
es flockt der Ruß, der Regen rinnt,
und langsam wächst das Buch.

HANOVER SQUARE

For sixteen weeks now we live (*sans* pension!)
in the little boarding-house;
for us there never shrills the phone,
soon poorer we'll be than our mouse.
The riff-raff hold their noses high
when passing our laundry nook:
the soot forms flakes, the rain runs by,
and slowly it grows the book.

Old wash-shrunk collars make it do
if forced by paper clip;
the ink brush for your high-heeled shoe
paints over its worn tip.
The junk dealer from your stuff he'll buy
the finest pieces, the crook:
the soot forms flakes, the rain runs by,
and slowly it grows the book.

Now rarely our kettle's a-spin
(of tea almost empty the tin!)
and fall-brown (when we moved here green!)
the little square's park looks in.
Occasionally, when an egg we fry,
the cat calls on the cook:
the soot forms flakes, the rain runs by,
and slowly it grows the book.

ZUHAUS IN LONDON

Wo der Sprung sich im Verputz verzweigt,
wo der Staub aus allen Dielen steigt,
trocknen heiser Schlund und Gaumen aus,
bin ich, fremd in London, still zuhaus.

Wo das Laub im Sommer grün verdorrt,
wo am Zinstag abfällt erst ein Wort,
bricht der Schweiß schon auf der Stiege aus,
bin ich, fremd in London, still zuhaus.

Wo der Milchmann früh die Flaschen bringt,
wo der Nebel durch die Ritzen dringt,
hustet sich der Ruß in Brocken aus,
bin ich, fremd in London, still zuhaus.

AT HOME IN LONDON

Where cracks in plaster-of-Paris maps past wars,
the dust of centuries ascends from all floors,
where hoarsely dry feel throat and tonsil's dome:
a stranger I'm in London, safe at home.

Where green this summer withers on the stalk,
where only on rent day downstairs there's small talk,
where in a sweat one breaks climbing stairs d'aplomb:
a stranger I'm in London, safe at home.

Where with the dawn the milkman still arrives,
where damp the fog through all the crannies drives,
one coughs up soot in lumps from coal debris:
a stranger I'm in London, safe at home.

DAS BLECHDACH

Mein Zimmer ist das höchste hier im Haus;
es streckt vorm Fenster sich ein Blechdach aus.

Die Jahre lasten auf mir altem Mann;
es sammelt sich auf ihm viel Unrat an.

Verputz und Staub, der Rost, der es zerfrißt,
der grün verdorrte, scharfe Taubenmist.

Papier, zerknüllt, von meinem Tisch und Fach.
Der Regen schlägt wie Erbsen hart aufs Dach,

der Nebel wird zum Reif, die Glut zum Stich;
so leben wir dahin, das Dach und ich.

THE TIN ROOF

My room's the topmost of the house I'm in,
and off the window there's a roof of tin.

The years they've put their weight on me old man;
a lot of junk's collected on its span.

The plaster and dust, the rust corroding it,
the green dried-up, sharp-smelling pigeon shit.

Thrown from my desk, a crumpled sheet of proof.
The London pea-soup rain hits hard the roof,

and fog turns rime, sun's blaze the brain does fry;
that's how we spend our lives, the roof and I.

DER KLEINE SQUARE

Wenig Raum gibt das Geviert für Spiel,
und das Strauchwerk heißt nicht eben viel;
doch die Bäume stehn von altersher,
als kein Haus noch stand, im kleinen Square.

Mitten in der dicht bewohnten Stadt
liegt er abseits; wer sein Heim hier hat,
kann hier ungestört sein, ja noch mehr,
lebt vergessen wie der kleine Square.

Und wo aus Getrieb im fremden Land
ich nach Jahren meine Zuflucht fand,
schaff ich wieder, und mir fällt's nicht schwer;
hab drum Dank, du stiller kleiner Square.

THE LITTLE SQUARE

There's not much space for games here in the park,
no fancy landscape gardener left his mark;
yet trees here breathe a centuries-old-air
from times no houses stood on the little square.

At London's dense-lived center it lies remote;
who has his home here his pipe in peace can smoke,
and even more, can live as if he were
forgotten by the war, like the little square.

And where from bedlam in a foreign land
I've found asylum, after years being banned,
I work again, regained my rhyming flair,
with thanks to you, my quiet little square.

FREMD IN LONDON

Im Speiseraum muffelt's, die Zunge verdorrt
beim Kaffee mir, und hart ist der Platz;
schon zahlen die anderen laut und gehn fort,
und jeder hier hat einen Schatz.

Auch andre sind Flüchtlinge, ich aber bin
in London ganz fremd . . . Es verhallt
das Geräusch in den Gassen, es zuckt mir das Kinn,
und das schwarze Geländer ist kalt.

Hab kein Geld und bin kränklich, in mir ist es still
seit Jahren; ich kann es verstehn,
daß kein Mädel mit mir was zu tun haben will,
doch allein muß noch heut ich vergehn.

Ich hab keine Arbeit, kein Heim, mir zerreibt
es im Leib das Gedärm . . . Was ich kann,
ist: Gedichte schreiben, wie keiner sie schreibt,
und brunzt auch kein Hund mich hier an.

ALL-NIGHT ESPRESSO

The lunchroom smells musty, the tongue's dried up
from coffee, and the hard bench-seat hurts;
already the others have paid for their cup
and left, all of them with girls called 'birds'.

Others are refugees, too, yet still
I'm alien in London . . . Loud street bazaars fold
their tents, when I leave, with my chin a-chill
and quivering, the black handrail feels cold.

I'm penniless, sick, years ago I withdrew
into stillness; now I can understand
why no girl here the night with me wants to do,
yet even today I hate solo to land.

I'm jobless, homeless, my stomach cramps bite
me apart . . . What I can do is this:
write poems like nobody else can write,
though no dog about that gives a piss.

DAS TELEPHON

Auf dem Square flirrt leer die Helle,
schwirrt seit Stunden nicht ein Ton;
durch das Glas der roten Zelle
gleißt das schwarze Telephon.

Nicht daß ich im Buch was fände;
drinnen ist es drückend heiß,
vollgekritzelt sind die Wände,
und es riecht nach Harn und Schweiß.

Und mich hält ein Schmerz, ein stummer,
namenlos in seinem Bann;
wüßt ich eine einzige Nummer
in der Stadt, ich rief' sie an.

THE PHONE BOOTH

Hot noon keeps the square in its lorn spell,
for hours there's no buzzing tone;
still through the glass of the red cell
there gleams the black telephone.

Not that I'd find any name in its book;
the heat inside is dripping wet,
the walls have an over-scribbled look,
and it smells of urine and sweat.

And the pain as if a speechless hummer
nameless keeps me in its stall;
if only I knew a single number
in London I'd make a call.

VERLASSENHEIT, VERLASSENHEIT . . .

Verlassenheit, Verlassenheit,
ist auch mein Leben leer,
ich finde dich doch allezeit
in meinem kleinen Square.
Du knarrst mir aus den Treppen zu
vor Nacht im Boardinghouse;
du bleibst mir, was ich laß und tu,
geht auch das Geld mir aus.

Du machst die Scheiben alle blind,
du tropfst aus Tank und Wann;
du wehst mich spät im schalen Wind
der Untergrundbahn an.
Du liegst gehäuft in Schutt und Staub,
bist im Asphalt zu schaun;
du treibst im grün verdorrten Laub
des Nachts durch Camden Town.

Ich seh dich als vergilbtes Gras,
als Sprung im Pflasterstein;
es schenkt im Pub der Wirt ins Glas
dich mir als Cider ein.
Du bist im grell bemalten Mund
der Huren auf dem Strich;
du bist in Londons ödem Rund
mir näher selbst als ich.

O LONELINESS, O LONELINESS

O loneliness, o loneliness,
although my life's stripped bare
I always have you around, I guess,
on my own little square.
You're creaking at the staircase well
at dusk at our boarding place;
you're always there, wherever I dwell,
though my money's gone without trace.

You've lent all panes their blackout tint,
you trickle from sink and tub;
you blow in my face the stale late wind
of London's underground hub.
You lie piled up in debris from eaves,
in asphalt's potholes brown;
you stir underfoot in dried-green leaves
at night through Camden Town.

I see you yellowed as the grass,
as cracked as cobblestone;
the publican pours you in my glass
of cider nursed alone.
You're on the garish-painted lips
of whores who jointly walk:
on miles of London's lonely strips
you're closer to me than my stalk.

41

IM HOCHHAUS

Ich geh kaum einmal in der Woche aus,
die Wohnung ist die höchste hier im Haus,
als Gast hab ich sie ganz für mich allein,
verworren hallt die Stadt zu mir herein.

Das Badezimmer ist für mich stets frei,
im Fach stehn die Konserven Reih an Reih;
der Ventilator fächelt, ist es schwül,
der Eisschrank hält Siphon und Fruchtsaft kühl.

So leb ich nun den ganzen Sommer schon,
die Schreibmaschine läuft mir fast davon;
und viel schon ist es, wenn die Wanduhr tickt
und wenn im Schacht der schwarze Aufzug klickt.

IN A HIGH-RISE FLAT

I'm going out maybe just once a week,
the flat's up in the sky, where off I sneak.
An absent owner's guest I'm not by choice,
what filters through to me is the city's noise.

The bathroom's always free just for myself,
canned food is lined up on the kitchen shelf;
the fan blows if outside it's sweltering hot,
for siphon & juice the icebox keeps a cool spot.

That's how I spend all summer like a recluse,
the typewriter almost runs away with my muse;
and what makes news here are the clock's loud ticks,
and when outside in the shaft the black lift clicks.

IN EINER UNTERGRUNDBAHNSTATION

Wie sie alle schlafen,
wie sie alle schlafen,
auf geflochtnen Matten ausgestreckt,
ihre Siebensachen
neben sich, den flachen
Leib mit Daun und Mänteln zugedeckt.

Schal streicht oft ein Saugen
durch den Schacht, die Augen
blinzeln bleiern im gedämpften Licht;
die nach langen Pausen
dumpf vorüberbrausen,
die schon späten Züge störn sie nicht.

Ihre kleinen Zimmer,
manches Ding, das Schimmer
lieh dem Leben, alles ist nicht mehr;
und die Beßres hätten,
aber hier sich betten,
ach, wie elend sind erst sie und leer.

Wie sie alle schlafen,
wie sie alle schlafen,
Mann Weib Kind geheiligt durch ihr Leid;
als die Dächer barsten
und der Stadt Verkarsten
anhob, war ich fern in Sicherheit.

Wo es riecht nach Asche,
wo ich nun mich wasche
früh im Finstern, bin ich ihnen nah,
will ich nicht die Gassen
dieser Stadt verlassen,
mag geschehn, was ihnen einst geschah.

IN AN AIR RAID SHELTER TUBE

How they all sleep,
how they all sleep,
stretched out on wicker chair mats,
their odds and ends
besides them like friends,
beneath their quilts, coats, and hats.

Stale drafts run oft
from air shafts aloft,
their eyes blinking under damped light;
no intermittent train's pause
from make-shifts can rouse
who sleep in interminal night.

Their bombed-out rooms,
what life there blooms,
in the sun, all that's no more;
and the upper classes
now mix with the masses,
forlorn like never before.

How they all sleep,
how they all sleep,
man wife child in their sanctuary;
when roofs burst like fountains,
and karstic turned London's
slums, I felt safe in my verse factory.

Where it smells of ash,
where off it I wash
this dark dawn, we are quite close,
don't want to leave
their streets but to grieve,
may happen what once did to those.

AUF EIN GRÜNES TRÜMMERFELD

Im Glast liegt zwischen Haus und Haus
das grüne Trümmerfeld;
man nimmt noch grad den Grundriß aus,
tief zwischen Strunk und Spelt.
Die Eisenträger rosten schon,
die morsche Planke glüht;
die Disteln starrn, es schwingt der Mohn:
es treibt und grünt und blüht.

Du Fleck voll Schutt und Feuerkraut,
ich fühl im fremden Land,
so oft mein Auge dich erschaut,
mich innerst dir verwandt.
Es stürzte das Gerüst mir ein,
längst bin ich ausgeglüht;
und doch muß noch gesungen sein:
es treibt und grünt und blüht.

Still war es lang, doch heute summt
der Tödel über dir;
und wenn er über dir verstummt,
dann ist es aus mit mir.
Schwarz schwirrt zu Häupten uns sein Wind,
der Sommer gleißt und glüht;
und wie wir auch zertrümmert sind,
es treibt und grünt und blüht.

ON A FIELD OF GREEN RUINS

In noon's glare between two blocks of flats spared
the field of green ruins lies;
the layout of buildings just being bared
between tree roots and spelt that fries.
The girders rust like *Luftwaffen* wings,
the rotten planks glow in their glooms;
the thistle bristles, the poppy swings:
it thrives, it greens, and blooms.

You lot of bloody trash and weeds,
I feel in my exile's chagrin,
whenever my memory your eyesore reads,
how deeply we're both akin.
The structure collapsed on me long ago,
burned out I've been like your rooms,
and yet what must be sung if low:
it thrives, it greens, and blooms.

There was a long pause, but humming today
there's a new deadly toy above you;
and when it stops overhead with its pay-
load, then all's over with me, too.
In black space above there whirs its wind
(and summer glistens and gloams!)
and even as we're about to be ruined:
it thrives, it greens, and blooms.

FREMD FÜR IMMER

Fremd für immer bleib ich hierzuland
und es hat das Herz mir ausgebrannt;
ach ich wünsch, ich könnt von meinem Leben,
eh es schwindet, irgendwas noch geben.

Von zu vielem, das ich einst vertan,
hebt in mir es sacht zu singen an;
gebt Gehör mir, Freunde, laßt euch bitten:
hätt ich sonst doch ganz umsonst gelitten.

Hör mich, Flüchtling, der du stempeln gehst,
hör mich, der du deine Sprache schmähst,
hör mich, dem sich nachts ergießt der Samen,
hört mich, ihr, bei euren hundert Namen.

Bleibt lebendig unter dicker Haut,
gleicht euch an, doch schluchzt im Mutterlaut,
sucht nicht Liebe nur für eine Stunde,
glaubt mir, glaubt, und geht nicht vor die Hunde.

Morgen, wenn es noch ein Morgen gibt,
dröhnt die Tenne, wird die Spreu gesiebt:
und im Takt mögt ihr mich wieder finden,
der ein Nichts schon heut ist vor den Winden.

ALWAYS A STRANGER

Always a stranger on this isle called home,
too much burned out to write another poem,
o, how I wish I could (while I'm still here!)
give what's in me before I disappear.

So many things I've wasted, my own thing
it softly starts again in me to sing:
lend me your ear, my friends, each be my witness,
that I've suffered not in vain unfitness.

Listen to me, refugees over here on the dole,
you who're jeering your accent to save your soul,
listen, you late at night in your wet dreams,
you, known by five score and more of pseudonyms.

Keep your thick skin, but to yourself belong,
adjust yourselves, yet sob in your mother tongue,
don't search for half-hour's love in London's fogs,
believe me, believe, and don't go to the dogs.

Tomorrow, if there'll be a new day's beat,
the chaff again is sifted from the wheat:
then you may find me in my rhyme reborn,
a nothing though today, in big winds forlorn.

ES MÖGEN ANDRE EINE HEIMAT SUCHEN . . .

Es mögen andre eine Heimat suchen,
ich bin von meiner für die Zeit verbannt;
ich bin nicht da zu preisen noch zu fluchen,
im Lärm der Stille bin ich zugewandt.

Die Sprache lern ich nicht, um zu gestalten;
es ist für mich genug, sie zu verstehn,
des fremden Landes Sitten einzuhalten.
Es drängt mich nicht, in ihnen aufzugehn.

Mein Auftrag, mir von Anbeginn gegeben,
im Mutterlaut, ist mir zur Zeit verhüllt;
ich kann ihn nicht enträtseln, nur erleben,
ihn, der sich einzig im Gedicht erfüllt.

Wenn wir einst kommen–und wir kommen wieder –
bin ich zu lernen, nicht zu lehren da,
fürs erste, mögen meine kleinen Lieder
auch heut schon singen, was mir einst geschah.

Es mögen andre suchen eine Bleibe,
und nützlich werden, der und jener reich;
doch wo ich steh und was ich immer treibe,
dort steht und lebt ein Stückchen Österreich.

OTHERS MAY BE LOOKING FOR A HOMELAND

There may be others looking for a homeland,
from my own I'm banned, for as long as it takes;
it's not for me to praise or curse offhand,
I'm tuned to noises that radio silence makes.

The English language I study not for inventing;
just enough for me to get the gist
of foreign customs here, not for consenting
or immersing myself as an able linguist.

My mission, given me from the beginning
in my mother tongue, is hidden from me at this time,
I can't decode it, only experience by winning
what reveals itself in a pure rhyme.

Till we return (and we'll be going home!)
I'm here to learn and not to teach any class.
For now I'm praying that this little poem
sings today what for me has come to pass.

There may be others searching for safe shelter,
reading for BBC's German desk at high fees,
yet where I make a living (if helter-skelter!)
of free Austria there'll be a small piece.

ALTE FREUNDE

Mein Bruder im Elend hier, reich mir die Hand;
der einzige bist du im frostigen Land,
der drückte mit mir in der Schule die Bank,
der weiß, dieser stotterte, jener war krank:
drum gehen wir gern noch eins trinken.

Und sahn in der Heimat einander wir nicht
seit Jahren, du hast noch das gleiche Gesicht;
dir brach man, bevor man dich wies aus dem Land,
das Mäusel, mir hat, was ich schrieb, man verbrannt:
drum gehen wir gern noch eins trinken.

Und ziehst, schwadronier ich, die Brauen du kraus,
und wächst dein Getu mir beim Hals schon heraus -
dich reißt's in den Gliedern, mich zwickt's im Gedärm,
es macht sich mit dir so beruhigend Lärm:
drum gehen wir gern noch eins trinken.

Und hatten auch unlängst erst wir einen Streit,
wie wärn wir gar elend, wärn nicht wir zu zweit;
dein Schädel wird kahl und mein Hals viel zu dick,
uns sitzt schon, mein Lieber, der Tod im Genick:
drum gehen wir gern noch eins trinken.

OLD FRIENDS

My brother in misery here, give me your hand;
the only one I've got in this cold land,
who shared the Vienna high school bench with me,
who knew this stutterer, that chronic absentee:
a very good reason to have a drink for the road.

And though we did not meet for many years
back home, you look still the same and touch me to tears;
they broke your elbow-joint before they let
you leave; they burned my scripts, not published yet:
a very good reason to have a drink for the road.

And if you frown at my friends in pretty high places,
and I get fed up with your often making clown's faces –
you with the pain in your joint, I in my gut,
with you I feel like making noise in our rut:
a very good reason to have a drink for the road.

And though not long ago we had fight,
we'd be miserable if we called it a night;
your skull gets baldish, and my turtleneck slack,
my friend, we constantly carry death on our back:
a very good reason to have a drink for the road.

PART III

ISLE OF MAN (1940)

AUF DER LORE

Es führt durch grüne Saaten
zu sechst uns über Land
die Lore; mit Soldaten
ist's ringsherum bemannt.
Die queren Bretter knarren,
die Fraun und Kinder starren
uns an vom Straßenrand.

Schlaff fühlt im Rock die Tasche
sich an, die barg den Paß;
schief sitzen Schlips und Masche,
die Augen sind uns naß.
Wir haben nichts zu sagen,
aufs Hemd nur, das wir tragen
am Leib, ist noch Verlaß.

Die kleinen Koffer schwanken,
sie haben kein Gewicht;
wir stemmen an die Planken
die Schuh und reden nicht.
Im Halse würgt der Bissen;
wohin wir fahren, wissen
selbst die Soldaten nicht.

Wo werden wir heut landen
zur Nacht und für wie lang?
Wie wird man uns gewanden,
gilt Stellung noch und Rang?
Wie werden wir dort wohnen?
Der Wind braust in den Kronen,
die Schatten werden lang.

ON THE LORRY

The lorry, through green crops,
takes six of us overland;
with Tommy soldier cops
it's all around us manned.
The boards creak of the fairing,
the women and children are staring
at us from the roadside rand.

In our coat the pockets
feel slack without the passport; askew our tie, from sockets
our eyes stream as if from gas.
Having nothing at all to say,
our shirt is all we may
keep on this roundup day.

The little suitcases shake,
they seem to carry no weight;
with shoes against crossboards they take
us West, and we silently wait.
On the navy chow we're choking,
even the soldiers do joking-
ly speculate on our fate.

Where shall we make landfall tonight
and for exactly how long?
What will our clothes be like,
to which class will we belong?
How shall we live there (*sans* tea shops?)
The wind roars through the treetops,
their shadows growing long.

DIE INTERNIERTEN VON HUYTON

Sie weckten uns aus unsern Betten
noch vor der ersten Hahnenkraht
und brachten uns aus vielen Städten
auf Autos hinter Stacheldraht.
Die Stunden schleichen grau verhangen,
wir stehn, getrennt von Kind und Weib,
mit unsern Köfferchen in Schlangen
und stehn die Bein uns in den Leib.
Wir sind die Huyton-Internierten,
getrennt von Schwungrad, Pult und Feld,
der erste Sieg der Alliierten,
das Salz und, ach, der Staub der Welt.

Dann gibt's die erste Lagerbrühe,
und endlich kommt man aus den Schuhn;
kein Stuhl, sind wir nach kleiner Mühe
schon schwach, lädt ein, drauf auszuruhn;
auf unserm Strohsack lümmelnd, stecken
beisammen wir, wie es sich traf,
und wenn wir in die rauhen Decken
uns einrolln, flieht uns lang der Schlaf.
Vorm Fenster dröhnt der Schritt der Posten,
ihr langgedehnter Zuruf gellt;
so ruhn im Westen und im Osten
von uns viel tausend schwarz umstellt.

Man kann gewiß nur jenen trauen,
die man von früher kennt, im Haus;
Gerüchte gehen um, das Grauen
malt käsig nachts die Wände aus;
der Atem stockt, die Pulse hämmern,
schlägt ungewohnter Laut ans Ohr;

THE HUYTON INTERNEES

They woke us up in our nightgowns,
before the first crow of a henhouse crier,
collecting us all from various towns
in homeguard lorries behind barbed wire.
The hours crawl as if gray blue,
we stand apart from wife and child,
with our small bags in a long queue,
patiently waiting, of dreams beguiled.
    We are the Huyton internees,
    thrown out of a wartime job,
    the first of the Allies' casualties,
    the salt of the Earth, o Lord.

Then there's the first arrival chow,
and at last they come off, our dirty shoes;
collapsing (no chair to rest on now!)
on a mattress . . . Starved of the evening news,
we stick together like flocks of sheep,
and rolled in rough blankets to cover the skin
for hours on end escapes us all sleep,
just thinking of what there could have been.
    In front of the window the sentinel
    yells his drawn-out challenge address;
    that's how in camps here (in the East they're hell!)
    thousands feel shadowed as if by SS.

You cannot entrust your life but guys
you've known once well outside these walls,
where rumors abound of fifth-column spies
and at night haunt the deadly pale halls;
you cannot breathe, your blood pressure's high,
when air-raid sirens are tested late;

vielleicht stehn bald im Morgendämmern
die Deutschen vor dem Schragentor.
Dann zerren sie uns an den Haaren
und stelln uns alle an die Wand;
und was im Hirn seit vielen Jahren
wie Rausch uns schmerzt, spritzt in den Sand.

's kann sein auch, daß nach vielen Wochen,
was uns bedroht, zerfällt, zerrrinnt;
dann blüht aus den verkohlten Knochen
der Mohn und wiegt sich rot im Wind.
Wie viele dann auch darum wissen,
wir aber wußten vor der Zeit
und sind berufen, mit zu hissen
die Fahne der Gerechtigkeit.
Dann braucht man uns, die Internierten,
auf die man wieder etwas hält;
dann baun wir mit den Alliierten
und Volk mit Volk die neue Welt.

maybe at daybreak soon there's a cry
as Nazi tanks smash through the gate.
    Then they'd be dragging us by the hair,
    and put us all against the wall;
    and (what has been for years our scare!)
    our brains stain the sand, should England fall.

But then again it could happen that
after many weeks the *Blitzkrieg* abates;
then out of charred bones the poppy red
shall sway at unguarded death-camp gates.
Like many others we'll be informed,
(we having fathomed what's in our soul!)
will be invited (when Vienna's stormed!)
to hoist freedom's flag high on the pole.
    Then they again need us internees,
    the folk on scrapheaps they've hurled:
    then after the Allies' victories
    together we'll build a brave new world.

NACH DER ZUWEISUNG DES ZIMMERS

Das wär der Raum, drei Meter lang, zwei breit;
stell ab dein Zeug, hier hausen wir zu zweit
fürs nächste, Freund, vielleicht für lange Zeit.

Die Risse ziehen sich, scheint's, durchs ganze Haus;
es riecht nach Tünche, Holz, doch nicht nach Maus.
Das Fenster geht auf den Verhau hinaus.

Gut wär es, wenn der Schrank ein Sperrschloß hätt;
vielleicht kommt noch für dich ins Eck ein Bett.
Das Sims dort gibt ein gutes Bücherbrett.

Wie teilen wir uns hier das Leben ein?
Ich schrubb den Flur, du hälst den Vorraum rein.
Ich laß dich, wenn du schreiben willst, allein.

Zur Ruhe bläst es . . . Rollcall ist um acht.
Hart ist der Keil, das Lager bald gemacht;
roll ganz dich ein und schlaf die erste Nacht.

Zu tun sein wird sonst eben hier nicht viel;
ich schreibe morgen um ein Damespiel.
Dies durchzuhalten ist das einzige Ziel.

AFTER ROOM ASSIGNMENT

So that's the space, three meters long, two wide;
just drop your stuff, we'll live here, side by side,
maybe for months, friend, riding out the tide.

The cracks extend, it seems, throughout the house;
it smells of whitewash, wood, but not of mouse.
Barbed-wire fences signal broken vows.

If only the cabinet had a lock and key;
we'll get a corner bunk for you maybe.
The sills make good shelves for a library.

How do we arrange the schedule for our small room?
I scrub the floor, you clean the hall with a broom.
I leave you alone with your writing, escaping the gloom.

The lights-out whistle blows . . . Roll call's at eight.
Our beds with wedge-shaped pillows soon are made.
Just wrap yourself tight, tonight's sleep won't come late.

To cope here with routine depends on your frame
of mind; tomorrow I'll send away for a game
of checkers. To see it through's our only aim.

SO LIEG ICH EIN ZWEI STUNDEN . . .

So lieg ich ein zwei Stunden
schon wach und schlaf nicht ein;
mich juckt die rauhe Decke,
es schnarcht wer in der Ecke
und krault im Schlaf sein Bein.

Der Kotzen, der vors Fenster
gespannt ist, hält nicht dicht,
vom Wachturm strähnig spuken
die Kegel durch die Luken
und blenden mein Gesicht.

Es hallt der Schritt der Posten,
der Wind seufzt durch den Spelt;
die Schriften sind verkommen,
die Freunde fortgeschwommen -
was soll ich auf der Welt?

TOSSING ABOUT FOR ONE, TWO HOURS

Tossing about for one, two hours,
still awake, and sleep won't come;
I'm itching from the blanket coarse,
somebody in the corner snores,
and in his sleep he's scratching his bum.

The worn-out rag across the window
can't be kept all tight in place;
the watchtower sweeps its ghostly light cones
through the gaps and over cheekbones,
flashing also over my face.

It echoes loud the march of the sentries,
the wind through the spelt sighs like a curse:
my writings fell to censor snippers,
my friends have left on ocean clippers –
what do I live for on this earth?

DAS HAFERFELD

Aus des Lagers letztem Winkel
geht es auf ein Haferfeld;
um die Gruben blüht der Dinkel
und im Stacheldraht der Spelt.

Auf dem Wachturm döst der Posten,
schultert lässig das Gewehr;
um die Scherben, um die Pfosten
flirrt die Luft versengt und leer.

Manchmal nach dem Mittagessen
flücht ich in das leere Haus,
starre stundenlag vergessen
übers satte Feld hinaus.

Durch die Wiesen laufen Hürden,
kleines Wirtshaus winkt am Saum;
Forken pressen grüne Bürden
und die Eichel tropft vom Baum.

Drüben wölbt in seiner Helle
sich das Leben sacht und groß;
reglos lieg ich auf der Schwelle
und verström in seinen Schoß.

THE CORN FIELD

Where the camp, shrunk to a corner,
borders on a cornfield belt,
around the pits aristae garner,
and in barbed wire blooms the spelt.

On the watchtower dozes the sentry,
shoulders his rifle loosely hinged;
around the shards at the foot of the gantry
noon's air glitters empty and singed.

After mess I sometimes escape
to the empty barrack room
and stare for hours at the landscape
beyond the ripened cornfield's glume.

Through the meadows there run hedges,
a small inn's smoke cloud waves at me;
the hay forks press down on green wedges,
and the acorns drop from the tree.

Over there at high noon's lumen
life's expanding, softly great;
unmoving I lie on its brink, a human
flowing through its mother gate.

ÜBER DEN STACHELDRAHT

Wir standen hinterm Gittertor
–wie war der Abend blau und klar!–
scharf schob der Stacheldraht sich vor
und wehrte unsrer kleinen Schar;
erst summte wer für sich allein,
wir andern fielen lauter ein.
Wie war der Abend blau und klar!

Ein dumpf Gebrumm, ein heller Klang
–wes war die Ziehharmonika?–
und plötzlich war im Überschwang,
mit dem wir sangen, alles da:
das alte Haus, das volle Glas,
die ferne Liebste, dies und das.
Das tat die Ziehharmonika.

Der Wachsoldaten zwei und drei
–der Wind ging durch den Ginster leis–
die hatten grad den Abend frei
und winkten userm kleinen Kreis;
sie legten draußen sich ins Gras
und sangen uns auf englisch was.
Der Wind ging durch den Ginster leis.

Und einer gar sang heiser dann
–blank floß der Glanz ums Gittertor–
die Lorelei und hielt bald an,
denn fluchend ging die Wache vor;
sie scheuchte uns zurück, doch lang
blieb noch im Ohr uns dieser Sang.
In Schatten schwand das Gittertor.

BEYOND THE BARBED WIRE

We stood behind the wrought-iron gate
–how blue and clear the evening sky!–
the sharp barbed wire would be its fate
if to escape this small group should try;
first humming solo, milling about,
then all of us joined in aloud.
How blue and clear the evening sky!

A growling deep, a glissando key
–what hidden accordion made us sing?–
and all of a sudden in ecstasy
there was it all, o, everything:
the old house, and lots of wine from the vat,
the distant sweetheart, this and that.
That's what the accordion made us sing.

Of sentries there were two or three
–the wind fanned softly a juniper tree–
by chance they had the evening free,
and waved at our small group at ease;
outside they lay in the grass, so young,
and something they sang, some English song.
The wind fanned softly a juniper tree.

And one of them even started some verse
–the moon washed white the camp gate's fence!–
of the Lorelei, but was stopped by a curse;
the watch chased us back, yet in the suspense
there echoed exiled Heine's song
in our ears the whole night long.
The gate in shadows was immersed.

69

ICH BIN VON FRÜH BIS ABEND MÜD . . .

Ich bin von Früh bis Abend müd . . .
seit Tagen weiß ich nicht die Zeit;
kaum merk ich, daß der Koks verglüht,
der Weg zum Tor ist mir zu weit.
Ich bin von Früh bis Abend müd.

Ich feg den Flur, ich kratz den Grind,
ich scheure Napf und Teller rein;
die Leut, die mit im Zimmer sind,
sie könnten mir nicht fremder sein.
Ich feg den Flur, ich kratz den Grind.

Ich steh zum Rollcall vor dem Haus,
ich tu, als wart ich auf die Post;
ich schreibe meinen Bogen aus
und würz mit Beefex mir die Kost.
Ich steh zum Rollcall vor dem Haus.

Ich mach wie andre mein Gesuch,
ich schreibe oft um mein Gepäck;
ich greif zu meinem Penguinbuch
und leg es schwindlig wieder weg.
Ich mach wie andre mein Gesuch.

Nachts lieg ich wach und kann nicht sehn,
was ich mir ausmal, Blust und Beer,
wie Cider glänzt, wie Frauen gehn;
ich kränk und sehn mich längst nicht mehr.
Nachts lieg ich wach und kann nicht sehn.

I AM FATIGUED FROM DAWN TILL DUSK

I am fatigued from dawn till dusk . . .
For days now I've lost count of time;
I hardly note the coke's dying husk,
my walk to the door seems more like a climb,
I am fatigued from dawn till dusk.

I sweep the floor, I scratch my scurf,
I scrub the dishes as if in a lab;
my roommates are getting on my nerve,
I couldn't care less about their gab.
I sweep the floor, I scratch my scurf.

I stand at roll call in front of the hut,
I act like others waiting for mail;
I fill in my sheet, which censors will cut,
and spice with Beefex the fare if stale.
I stand at roll call in front of the hut.

Like others I make my formal requests,
I often complain about my lost bag;
I pick up my Penguin reader for tests,
and put it away when with headache I gag.
Like others I make my formal requests.

At night wide awake I can't see in the dark,
what I imagine are blossoms and berries,
how cider sparkles, how women walk;
I'm ailing and long not for those once cherished.
At night wide awake I can't see in the dark.

DREI GRÜNE BÄUME

Drei Grüne Bäume
stehn auf der Halde
vor unserm Fenster
im fahlen Gras;
versperrt die Weiten
mit Draht und Stacheln,
gespickt die Mauern
mit Scherbenglas.

Drei grüne Bäume
in ihrem Schatten–
ein Strich zu Mittag,
am Abend breit–
verträumen schweigend
mit feuchten Augen,
mit fest geschloßnen,
wir unsre Zeit.

Drei grüne Bäume.
sonst nichts als Pfosten
und Schutt und Scherben
und Stacheldraht;
fern hinterm Lager
blühn Mohn und Raden,
es rauscht die Sichel,
es reift die Saat.

THREE GREEN TREES

Three green trees
stand on the scree,
outside our window
in fallow grass:
our vistas barred
by wire and barbs,
the walls being topped
by bits of glass.

Three green trees:
their shade at noon
a single line,
at sundown wide–
we silently dream
with tear-wet eyes
quite tightly closed,
our time we bide.

Three green trees:
nothing else but posts,
and rubble and shards,
and fence-barbed thorn;
behind the camp
bloom poppy and cockle,
the sickle swishes,
it ripens the corn.

Drei grüne Bäume:
Wir sind vergessen,
was wir verloren,
wir finden's nie;
bald birst der Himmel,
zerreißt's den Rasen,
fällt Eisenregen
vielleicht auf sie.

Drei grüne Bäume,
und noch nach Jahren
spüren wir Trauer
und Zorn im Blut,
das singt, es waren
in diesem Lande
drei grüne Bäume
allein uns gut.

Three green trees:
we are forgotten,
what we have lost
shall never return;
the heavens soon burst
to tear up the lawn,
falls a rain of acid
perchance they'll burn.

Three green trees,
in years to come
we'll still feel the grief
and rage that torments
our blood and sings:
there were in this land
just three green trees,
our only friends.

UND DER ABEND IST LANG . . .

Und der Abend ist lang
und es fällt schon das Laub
und vorm Haus ist uns bang
und der Wind schleift den Staub
und der Wachturm rückt nah
und es schwindet das Licht
und der Posten ist da
und der Drahtverhau dicht.

Und der Strohsack riecht dumpf
und der Polster ist schlecht
und das Brom macht uns dumpf
und doch schmerzt das Gemächt
und wir finden nicht Ruh
und Verbot steht aufs Licht
und wir raunen uns zu
und wir fürchten uns nicht.

Und die Heimat ist fern
und dies Dasein ein Dreck
und wir helfen uns gern
und es hat einen Zweck
und wir kommen einst frei
und wir wissen nicht, wann,
und wir warten seit Mai
und auf uns kommt es an.

AND EVENING TIMES CRAWL

And evening times crawl
and of fear there's a hint
and autumn leaves fall
and there's dust in the wind
and the watchtower looms
and it fades the light
and the sentry's voice booms
and the fence is barbed tight.

And the straw mat smells dank
and the bolter's a turd
and the mind's bromide blank
and your balls still hurt
and our souls don't find peace
and late-lights-on's a risk
and we watch the police
and we fear not their frisk.

And our homeland's no mother
and this life's full of shit
and mates help each other
and it pays to do it
and we're free some day
and we don't know when
and we've been waiting since May
and what counts is our yen.

AN MEINE MUTTER

Auf und nieder gehn vorm Zaun die Posten
und durchs Lager schleift den Staub der Wind;
schweigsam schweift mein feuchter Blick nach Osten,
wo die Maische nun vom Preßbaum rinnt.
Meine Habe ging daheim verloren;
wozu, Mutter, hast du mich geboren,
wenn die Weiten mir verrammelt sind?

Under deinen Augen, die nie trogen,
wuchs ich lässig auf dem Land heran;
vom Studieren ward ich eingezogen,
halb ein Bub noch und schon halb ein Mann.
An die Front marschierten wir geschlossen
und es ward mir das Gesicht zerschossen,
daß das Blut mit aus der Zunge rann.

Wochen durfte ich bei dir verbringen,
Schlund und Lungen wurden wieder heil,
und ich meinte, von den guten Dingen
würde nun auch mir mein volles Teil.
Allzugern nahm ich, was mir gebührte;
für die Armen stand ich ein und führte
still die schmale feder wie ein Beil.

Meine Schriften konnt ich nicht verschonen,
als man meinesgleichen schlug und stach;
wieder, Mutter, mußt bei dir ich wohnen,
und man sah dir nicht die Abkunft nach.
Autrecht, blauen Munds, mit grauen Haaren,
bliebst du, und ich mußte es erfahren,
daß es dir an Milch und Obst gebrach.

TO MY MOTHER

Off the fence the sentries their parameter pace,
and gusts sweep through the isle's internment camp,
in mute repost with moist eyes east I face,
where mash now into vats the presses stamp.
All my belongings way back home got lost:
for what, mother dear, into life have I been tossed,
when all the vistas now are blocked for this tramp?

Under your eyes, which never lied to me,
I grew up among our rural doctor's clan;
from studies away I was drafted (classed infantry!)
still half a boy, and already half a man.
Marched to the Russian front at a close-order pace,
that's where I got shot up, right in the face,
blood running out of my tongue while I still ran.

For weeks they let me stay home under your wings
(my gullet and lungs healed, but mothers you can't
        fool!)
and I was thinking of getting my share of good things
by taking my rightful place at life's higher school;
there standing up for poor folks, its whores on town's
        brink,
my first verse I happily saw in newspaper ink,
and wielded my small pen like a carving tool.

I couldn't save my writing from the green censor
while my kind was beaten and stabbed for shame;
again, mother, I stayed with you, when life became
        tenser,
and the brownshirts checked out your maiden name.
Upright, blue-lipped and gray-haired, my widowed mater,
you carried on; from neighbors I found out much later
how you saved on fruit and milk for your son of fame.

Übers Meer, das hinterm Grenzpfahl blaute,
kam ich her und dich ließ ich allein,
spielte darts; das Land, dem ich, vertraute,
gab mir Brot und sperrte mich dann ein.
Dasig rauscht das Blut mir in den Ohren;
wozu, Mutter, hast du mich geboren,
kann ich nirgends froh und friedsam sein?

Dumpfer schnellt es und es schmeckt nach Schimmel.
wo die schönen Balsaminen stehn;
Eisenregen fällt vom schwarzen Himmel,
und ich werd dich, Mutter, nie mehr sehn.
Singen will ich gerne durch die Schwaden
laut den nahm und fernen Kameraden,
und es kann kein Leids mehr mir geschehn.

Overseas, which blued beyond some boundary post,
I left you behind to play a game of darts;
the England I trusted as my freedom's host,
first fed me, then had me arrested, a man of rhymed arts.
High blood pressured now, why, mother, won't I ever
be happily working at some peaceful endeavour
when surrounded by aged Brit home guards?

The puff-balls mildewy tasting spores let fly,
where beautiful touch-me-nots bloom in the scree;
the acid rain comes down from the black sky,
and, mother, never again you I shall see.
I'll gladly be singing through the chemical fumes
for comrades near and far at camp shower rooms . . .
And nothing bad any more can happen to me.

WAS SOLL ICH DIR DENN SCHREIBEN

Was soll ich dir denn schreiben,
ich komm vom Flur-Aufreiben
in meinem blauen Schurz;
es sind, um zu verweilen,
die vierundzwanzig Zeilen,
die mir nur zustehn, viel zu kurz.

Ich brauch ein Hemd, ein Kissen,
und Schuh; ich laß dich wissen,
was ankam, was ich schrieb.
Kein Zensor, der die Tinten
durchliest von vorn und hinten,
soll lesen, daß ich dich noch lieb.

Nichts von der kahlen Stube,
nichts von des Strobsacks Grube . . .
vorm Fenster glänzt der Kies;
der Ginster blüht im Gatter,
doch nie stockt das Geschnatter
der alten Leute vom release.

Der Staub schlieft durch die Gassen;
würd, Schatz, ich heut entlassen,
mir bangte früh und spät,
du wärst in deiner Süße,
Mund, Wangen, Brüst und Füße,
mit Staub und Stacheldraht besät.

WHAT DO I WRITE YOU FOR

What do I write you for,
just after scrubbing the floor
in my blue-apron dress;
what both of us still binds
is but the twenty-four lines
I'm allowed, no more, no less.

I need a shirt, a pillow,
and shoes, no long megillah,
what arrived I let you know.
What I wrote no censor's brush
shall kill, though ladies may blush:
that I still love you so.

Forget about my bare room,
about exiled Heine's straw gloom
from windows bright sand one sees;
the juniper grows at the fence,
yet never the chattering ends
of old folks about their release.

The dust sweeps barrack streets, luv;
if today they'd let me off,
then always around you I must
be worrying that you, my sweet,
your mouth, cheeks, breasts, and feet
crawl with vermin and dust.

Beim Schreiben und beim Essen
und Schreiten einst, vergessen
werd ich es nie und nie,
daß man die Kameraden,
die besten, mir verladen
auf Loren hat wie Stücker Vieh.

Der Bogen geht zu Ende,
es zittern mir die Hände,
zerflossen ist die Schrift;
versuch, mich zu besuchen,
wir haben morgen Kuchen,
wenn man mich nicht vor Früh verschifft.

While writing and while lunching,
taking walks gravel-crunching,
I'll never forget how my best
camp comrades were shipped like cattle
in port-bound lorries that rattle
to Australia as the King's guest.

This letter has come to an end,
which to you I'm about to send
with shaking hands, ink's dripped;
come, try to visit me,
tomorrow we'll have some tea,
if at daybreak I won't be shipped.

LIED FÜR VERBANNTE

Horch, wie der Staub vorm Fenster rennt,
Frost wird die Nacht heut bringen;
bevor das Feuer niederbrennt,
will ich noch einers singen,
vom Volk daheim, von groß und klein,
vom weißen Wein, vom roten Wein,
den beißen in den Schenken,
die unsresgleichen henken.

Verboten ist der alte Bund,
verbrannt sind Band und Schriften;
des Volks ist nichs das Korn im Grund,
das Vieh nicht auf den Triften.
Ein Tick läuft durch die Tausendhand,
die tut das gleiche unverwandt;
die so geschwächten Seelen
sind lüstern nach Befehlen.

Es ist für uns hier, fremd, verstreut,
die Zeit noch nicht gekommen;
es ist schon viel, wann wir wie heut
einmal zusammenkommen.
Was nächtens an Propellern schallt,
hat zu zerstören nur Gewalt;
wir aber sind die Erben,
wir dürfen noch nicht sterben.

SONG FOR EXILES

Hear the dust run by the window,
frost the night will bring;
before the fire burns to a cinder
one more song I'll sing,
of folks back home, the tall and small,
of taverns where white and red wine are all
being tasted by those very fellows
who are killing our own on the gallows.

They've even outlawed the old printers' guild,
burned books as if cheap matches;
the people are robbed of their very own field
and cattle on steep green patches.
A tic runs throgh the millipede
on children's minds as well to feed;
thus weakened the souls in a trance
they greedily follow commands.

To us here, enemy aliens, they say,
our time has not yet come;
it means a lot that we today
can meet again to hum . . .
V-2 bombs that propel night's air
we must survive to be their heir;
they home in before they growl,
but we can't die like fowl.

Wie wir, vergessen und veriert,
hier um die Asche kauern,
die Laute, die ich schlag, sie wird
uns alle überdauern,
die Schar, die sich mit Blut bestäuft,
das Band, das durch die Halls läuft;
nun laßt uns still entfernen,
ein Frost klirrt von den Sternen.

As we, forgotten and forlorn,
here crouch at ashes' pall,
the zither that I strum near morn,
it will survive us all:
the gang of leeches, drugged with blood,
our bond run through this hall, by God;
now quietly let us get lost,
from stars there clinks a frost.

WIR HABEN NICHT ZEIT

Wann werden in Frankreich die Engländer landen,
wann haun das verbogene Kreuz wir zuschanden?
Wir warten und planen, die Heimat ist weit,
die Nachrichten fehln, und wir haben nicht Zeit.

Wir haben nicht Zeit, und wir haben es über,
die meisten von uns sind schon Vierzig und drüber;
man stellt sich mit Fünfzig so leicht nicht mehr um
und schafft noch . . . doch wer von uns bliebe gern
        stumm?

Das seinige hätte noch jeder zu leisten,
zu stehn wo er stand, auszumisten die meisten,
zu raten auch noch, wann das Umkrempeln ruhl;
wer hat schon ein Kind, das dies Werk für ihn tut.

Und dann möchte jeder noch gern etwas treiben,
was lang er sich wünschte; der eine möcht schreiben,
der andre möcht schnitzen und Grundbirnen ziehn,
der dritte ein wenig noch streunen in Wien.

Wir schneiden aus Heften Tabellen und Karten,
wir lauschen dem Ansager abends und warten;
wir tun unser Tagwerk, die Heimat ist weit,
das Heut zehrt uns aus und wir haben nicht Zeit.

LIVING ON BORROWED TIME

When will the English land in France,
when smash the swastika in a trance?
We wait and plan, for the homeland we pine,
no messages, we're living on borrowed time.

We don't have much time, we've got it up here,
a majority of forty-and-over we're;
at fifty yourself you don't lightly uproot,
but who of us would like to stay mute?

Each of us still has his thing to do,
and make his stand, when the weed-out anew
starts; we counsel each other and wait:
who after all has a son for a mate?

And then each of us has a dream come to light,
for which he's long hoped: one music to write,
the other whittle, plant a bean-green antenna . . .
the third (via time machine!) revisit Vienna.

We're clipping from journals graphs and maps
        well dated,
we monitor broadcasts, for which we've waited;
we toil far from home, we brave the clime,
we eat our heart out, living on borrowed time.

LIED DER DEPORTIERTEN

Der Melder kam vorm Tee gelaufen
und rief die ersten aus dem Haus,
wir fanden uns in wirren Haufen
und fragten bang einander aus;
dann rollten wir die rauhen Decken,
die Koffer schafften wir geschwind
zur Waage; mit den Kanevassäcken
stehn wir vorm Zelt im Abendwind.
    Sie lassen uns verschiffen
    beim ersten Schein des Lichts,
    nach Übersee verschiffen
    mit einem Sack ins Nichts.

Wie auch ein jedes arme Luder
verstört durchs Camp zum Captain rennt,
es wird der Bruder doch vom Bruder,
vom Vater doch der Sohn getrennt;
den Frauen wird das Herz es brechen,
vielleicht sehn wir die lieben nie,
und wenn sie uns auch viel versprechen,
was ist denn schon ein Internee?!
    Sie lassen uns verschiffen
    beim ersten Schein des Lichts,
    nach Übersee verschiffen
    mit einem Sack ins Nichts.

SONG OF THE DEPORTEES

The dispatcher came running just before tea,
and from the barrack called the first batch out;
just milling around for informal inquiry
we worried what this call was all about;
but then we rolled up our blankets in packs,
our few belongings quickly we prepared
for the navy scale; with canvas bags on our backs
we stand near the tent, cold-evening aired.
    They'll ship us out, I say,
    by convoy overseas,
    at first light of the day,
    with one sack and no reprieve.

Some poor wretch runs across camp all abother,
appealing his case at the Captain's hut –
kid brother be split from older brother,
the bond between father and son will be cut;
women's heart will break from broken promises,
maybe the loved ones we shall never again see.
And though they've promised a lot, the Tommies –
what's special about an internee?
    They'll ship us out, I pray,
    by convoy overseas,
    at first light of the day,
    with one sack and no reprieve.

Im Wind, der an den wirren Haaren
uns reißt, so stehn wir ratlos da,
wir wissen nicht, wohin wir fahren,
Australien oder Kanada.
Was wird man dort mit uns beginnen,
wo's feucht vielleicht steigt aus dem Grund,
wo tief vielleicht im Lande drinnen
die Glut uns sengt den Nachen wund?
    Sie lassen uns verschiffen
    beim ersten Schein des Lichts,
    nach Übersee verschiffen
    mit einem Sack ins Nichts.

Lebt wohl, ihr rostig grünen Hütten,
leb wohl, verdorrtes Distelfeld!
Seht, Freunde, wie sie uns verschütten,
das Salz und, ach, den Staub der Welt.
Mag's dem und jenem auch nicht passen,
wir kehren wieder, Mann und Sohn,
und sehn einst noch in Schutt die Gassen,
zerstört das Land, aus dem wir flohn.
    Wir werden uns verschiffen
    einst, England, aus dem Nichts
    und steigen aus den Schiffen
    im Schein des neuen Lichts.

In the wind, which tears at our wild hair,
we are baffled who'll go or stay,
since nobody told us where the hell we'll fare,
the Australian or the Canadian way.
What will they do with us for a new start,
help drill for oil in permafrost deep,
or in the desert heat with just one quart
of brackish water herding flocks of sheep?
    They'll ship us out with pay,
    by convoy overseas,
    at first light of the day,
    with a sack and no reprieve.

Farewell, you sea-green, rusty huts,
farewell, you dried-up thistle field!
They scatter us, friends, like dust and suds,
the salt of the earth, the world's future shield.
Though some fifth columnists would not agree
that sons and fathers will one day return,
our bombed-out flat again we will see,
the country we fled, still smolder and burn:
    Some day we'll ship out, save
    our souls from nothingness,
    a landing craft's first assault wave,
    a new day's light to bless.

ENTLASSUNG

Kaum geht noch wer im Office aus und ein,
die Fensterscheiben spiegeln leeren Schein,
bald wird das Lager ganz verlassen sein.

Was bleiben wird: der schwarzen Kreise zehn,
wo vor den Hütten heut die Kessel stehn,
Dachpappefetzen, die im Wind sich drehn.

Was bleiben wird: um neun Ühr Schläfrigkeit,
zum Tor, bei der Entlassung, das Geleit,
im Munde der Geschmack von Bitterkeit.

Vielleicht bleibt lang noch ein Gespräch im Sinn,
vielleicht bleibt, nur sich selbst zu traun, Gewinn;
für eine härtre Zeit war's ein Beginn.

DISCHARGE

The traffic at the office now has all but stopped,
the window panes shine blank, the empty floors look
      mopped,
the camp an air of desolation seems to adopt.

What will remain on the green just ten black circular cuts
of kettles standing now in front of vacant huts,
and loosened tar-roof panels twisting windward in spots.

What will remain: the nine o'clock yawn as if a cramp,
on discharge an escort to the exit, a good-bye, camp!
The taste in our mouths from suicidal bitterness damp.

Maybe some talks with friends will linger in your mind,
maybe what stays is trusting in yourself, the kind
of training needed for a coming harder grind.

PART IV

SLUMS AND BLACK BLACK COUNTRY (1942-43)

BLACK COUNTRY

Das Schrundenfeld zwischen den Städien
ist nirgends ganz richtiges Land;
zwar Heidekraut, Ginster und Kletten
begleiten die Straßen am Rand,
doch schwarz schuppt im Tal sich die Sohle
und schwarz schleicht dahin sich der Fluß;
denn unter dem Rasen ist Kohle
und über den Hügeln schwebt Ruß.

Es rosten im Grase die Loren,
es stehen die Schlote in Reihn,
es schneiden die Narben und bohren
sich tief ins Schiefergestein.
Es füllt der Wind alles Hohle
mit knirschendem schwärzlichem Grus;
denn unter dem Rasen ist Kohle
und über deb Hügeln schwebt Ruß.

Es leuchtet der Hochöfen Schwelen,
beginnt sich der Tag zu verziehn;
es treiben in trüben Kanälen
die trächtigen Barken dahin
und stocken an jeder Bohle,
als wär an der Schleuse es Schluß,
denn unter dem Rasen ist Kohle
und über den Hügeln ist Ruß.

BLACK COUNTRY

The fissured field between town and town
looks nowhere like real land;
even though heather, gorse and burdock abound
accompanying streets on their rand.
But black sheds cover the valley's floor,
and the river crawls black to boot;
for under the surface of coal is a core,
and over the hills floats soot.

The lorries have rusted in the grass,
the smokestacks point up in line,
the scars cut deeply into the slate
as sharply as carbonized glass.
The wind fills in the crevices and more
with crunchy and blackish coal's glut;
for under the surface of coal is a core,
and over the hill floats soot.

The sky still highlights the blast-furnace coke,
when dawn starts to wash out its glow;
the barges pregnant with their load
on oily canals stop to poke
around each pile encountered *en route*
as if the gate's locked for good;
for under the surface there's coal, rich loot,
but over the hills floats soot.

LOB DES PUBS

Gelobt sei mir in diesem frostigen Lande,
wo feucht die Luft stets ist und trüb das Licht,
der einzige Ort, in dem es keine Schande,
wenn eins von selbst zu seinem Nachbarn spricht.
Gelobt sei mir von Herzen jederzeit
das alte Pub für seine Freundlichkeit.

Wie tröstlich ist's zu wissen, daß vom Fasse
es *Cider* gibt, daß *Gin* und *Whisky* hier
in Flaschen stehen, und das *Ale,* das blasse,
ins Glas gepumpt wird und das bittre Bier.
Es ist willkommen, wem es hier genügt
und wer sich willig in die Ordnung fügt.

Wie friedlich lockt es draußen einen jeden,
wenn aus dem Pub die ersten Lichter flirrn,
wo von der Leber weg die Leute reden
und scharf die Pfeile an das Dartboard schwirrn.
Was er tagsüber für sein Ansehn tut,
hier pfeift der Mensch darauf und fühlt sich gut.

Des Tages zweimal nur, für ein paar Stunden,
darf diese gute Stätte offen sein;
doch wer da plant, durch Kinder und durch Runden
von Malzmilch und von Tee sie zu entweihn,
der bleibe gram sich selber allezeit
und finde nirgendwo Geselligkeit.

PRAISE OF PUBS

Singing its praise I'm in this frosty land,
where always the air in damp, and the light is pale,
of the only place, where it's no shame to stand
and talk to neighbors nursing pints of ale.
Heartily always be praised the friendly warm light
of the old pub from six to ten at night.

How good to know that cider's dispensed *en masse*
from kegs, that gin and whisky's bottled here,
and ale, the pale one's pumped into your glass
as is the dark-brown bitter English beer.
He is welcome, who into this system fits,
and to its order willingly submits.

How peaceful from the outside does it look,
when in the pub the first few lights are stirring,
where people speak their mind, by hook or crook,
and sharp the darts into the board are whirring.
A bloke here gives no damn, and feels real good
about what someone does for his livelihood.

Twice a day, for four brief drinking hours,
they may keep open the old tavern's gate;
but he who plans (with children's milk, which sours
the air, and malt or tea!) to desecrate
this public place, should feel ashamed, and flee
this last male bastion of true friends' company.

FISH AND CHIPS

Fish und Chips, eine Tüte voll, das war mein Mahl,
hatte Mutter drei Pennies für mich;
und im Zimmer die Luft war so dumpfig und schal,
daß das Tageslicht stockend verblich.
Ich kaute die knusprigen Krusten
und sog von den Fingern das Fett;
von drinnen kam quälendes Husten,
dort lag die Mutter im Bett.

Fish and Chips, eine Tüte voll, die bringt mein Schatz,
wann die Nebel die Gassen durchziehn;
in dem muffigen Durchgang ist nachts nicht viel Platz,
ist Platz nur für mich und für ihn.
Wir haben im Stehen uns gerne,
ich spür, wenn ich so ihn umfaß.
wie's mich sticht in der Brust, und die Sterne
verschwimmen, die Augen sind naß.

Fish and Chips, eine Tüte voll, die gibt's zuhaus,
wenn die Erde man häuft über mir,
für jedes von euch als mein' Leichenschmaus,
für jedes von euch auch ein Bier.
Hatt ich wenig, ihr Leute, vom Leben,
mir bangt nicht vorm Jüngsten Tag;
Fish and Chips wird im Himmel es geben,
Fish and Chips, so viel ich nur mag.

FISH AND CHIPS

Fish and chips, in a paper bag, that was my treat,
spent mother's three pennies on that;
and the air in the room that locked out the street,
was so dank that the daylight paled flat.
I chewed up the crispy brown stuff,
and sucked the fat from my finger;
from the back came a racking cough,
where my mother in bed did linger.

Fish and chips, in a paper bag, is what my lover
brings me, when fog sweeps the streets;
the musty passage fits me and my shover,
when he makes love to my tits,
We like doing it standing up,
though a stab in my chest a tear draws,
as his hand slips beneath my bra's cup;
ablur above us the stars.

Fish and chips, in a paper bag served for my sake,
when they shovel the earth on me dear,
for all of you a bite at my wake,
for each of you, too, a beer.
Though little I got out of life,
I fear not the Lord's Judgment Day;
on fish and chips in heaven they strive,
fish and chips, as much as I may.

AUF EINEN VOGELBEERBAUM
IN STAFFORDSHIRE

Brennroter Baum vor meinem Haus,
es zuckt mir schwach das Kinn;
daß du so schön herübergleißt
zu mir, ist nur, weil du nicht weißt
daß ich nicht britisch bin.

Wann mit dem Jahr vorm Haus die Welt
zu End mir schien als Kind,
dann wiesest seltsam, rot bepackt,
den Weg du übers Joch mir nackt
im herbstrauchblauen Wind.

Und sah ich auf der Wanderschaft,
schon müd, gespreizt dich stehn,
so schlang ich um die Hand ein Gras,
das schnitt, und summte dies und das,
und konnte weitergehn.

Sie wiesen mich aus meinem Land,
lang her ist's; mir geschah,
daß mir ertaubten Sinn und Ohr
und ich mich hierzuland verlor,
bis ich dich wiedersah.

Wir müd ich bin auch, meine Zeit
ist, Baum, noch nicht zu End;
mir steht ein Weiser irgendwo
und wirft zum Himmel, groß und schloh,
die aufgeregten Händ.

TO A ROWAN TREE IN STAFFORDSHIRE

You firebrand tree in front of my house,
my chin slightly quivers forlorn;
the reason why you so gloriously glow
for me, is only that you don't know
that I'm not British born.

When–like the year–the house did seem
the world's end to a barefooted *Kind,*
then you strangely packed with berries red,
for me were a mountain-pass sign that led
me across in autumnal blue wind.

And if tired out on my Odyssey,
I saw you straddling proud,
then I wrapped around my hand a green blade,
that cut, and hummed a time in your shade,
and could go on, cured of doubt.

They turned me out of my own land
long ago; what happened then
was that deafened by foreign signs and sound
I here wandered aimlessly around
till I saw you burning again.

Though tired I am, what's left me of time
isn't yet at an end of road's bends;
somewhere a signpost stretches up, without fail,
to heaven (huge and totally pale!)
excitedly its hands.

Er teilt den Weg, es ist ein Weg,
den muß ich einst noch gehn,
der ich hier niedrig steh im Licht;
die Leut und Dinge kenn ich nicht,
die wohl am Ende stehn.

Sind es die Freunde, die zum Wein
mir reichten oft das Brot?
Ist es verworrn die alte Stadt,
die nichts Bekanntes an sich hat,
und dort ein Knüppeltod?

Weiß ich auch nicht, was mir noch winkt,
beheimnisvolle Frucht:
lebendig ward ich wiederum
im fernen Land und beug mich stumm
in mir der schönen Wucht.

It parts the way for me, a fork
that still I must bend straight,
me standing low here in the light;
don't know the people and things that might
at tunnel's end for me wait.

Are they my friends who oft did wine
and dine me just on bread?
Is it all strange to me my town,
where people on re-visitors frown,
and cudgel them brain dead?

Though ignorant still of what's my fate,
o, mysterious rowan tree fruit:
alive again I became far from home;
I bow to you, devoting this poem
in me to our common root.

DIE DOWNS

Wo südlich der Stadt sich am sanfteren Rand
der Felder zerklüftet das kreidige Band,
ist plotzlich das Gras nicht mehr saftig und weich,
da heben sich kahl, nur mit wenig Gesträuch
und krüppligen Eichen die Downs.

Kein Ackerrain gibt da der Weide ihr Maß,
es rupfen die Schafe das schartige Gras,
es scharren die wilden Kaninchen im Bau,
und hoch hält, ein heiserer Schatten, im Blau
der Bussard sich über den Downs.

Der Ginster blüht gelb, und die Disteln stehn kraus,
und kommt aus der Stadt tags ein Paar hier heraus,
so fühlt es wie Brausen die Stille im Blut,
und niemand rings kümmert sich drum, was es tut
im wuchernden Farnkraut der Downs.

THE DOWNS

Where south of the town at the field's gentler rim
the chalk cliffs are fissured grayish-grim,
all of a sudden sappy grass turns dry;
and where stunted oaks set off the sky
and bushes, there are the Downs.

No boundaries here the pasture does keep,
only jagged grass-blades are plucked by the sheep,
wild rabbits scrape their burrows together,
and (a hoarse-screeching shadow!) high in the ether
a buzzard hangs over the Downs.

The gorse blooms yellow, the thistle runs wild,
and courting couples from town are beguiled;
for the silence here fills with a rush their blood,
and nobody cares who's doing what
in the rampart weeds of the Downs.

PART V

GUILDFORD CAMPUS (1943-45)

HEIMWEH NACH LONDON

Nicht Stadt noch Land ist der verfluchte Flecken,
in dem ich Unnütz endlich Arbeit fand;
ich fröstle unter meinen sieben Decken
und fühl mich hier zum zweiten Mal verbannt.
    Wo abertausend meinesgleichen sind,
    wo sacht der Mörtel von den Simsen rinnt
    und aus dem Basement nachts die Katzen schrein,
    in London möcht ich gerne wieder sein.

Im Blackout komm ich aus dem Schulgebäude
und kriege nirgendswo ein warmes Mahl;
sie sehn im Pub mich an, als hätt ich Räude,
der Wein ist teuer und der Cider schal.
    Wo schal es aus der Untergrundbahn weht,
    wo noch geschminkt ein leichtes Mädchen steht,
    im Staub der eingestürzten Häuserreihn,
    in London möcht ich gerne wieder sein.

Blau schwillt, rück ich die Bücher, das Geäder
mir an, kaum hab ich ihre Reihen lieb;
ich führ als wie ein Beil die schmale Feder
und weiß heut nicht mehr, was ich gestern schrieb.
    Wo, wann der Kessel summt, der Nebel wallt
    und feucht vom Tee ruft durch den Fensterspalt,
    und tausend wohnen Wand an Wand allein,
    in London möcht ich gerne wieder sein.

HOMESICK FOR LONDON

Not urban or rural is this bloody town,
where the ex-internee at last some work has found;
I shiver under seven quilts of down,
and for the second time I'm exile-bound.
    Where many thousands live of my own kind,
    Where mortar softly runs from wind-eyes blind,
    and cats at night in basements cry in vain,
    in London I would like to be again.

I emerge from campus in blackouts pale as chalk
to catch in vain warm food like a stray cat;
in pubs they treat me like a mangy dog,
the wine's expensive and the cider's flat.
    Where stale it blows from tube trains running late,
    where made-up tarts at shelter exits wait,
    in the debris of blitz-ruins down the lane
    in London I would like to be again.

My hand hurts when the books I shelve in school,
can't imagine that once I loved what now I hate;
my pen I hold like an engraver's tool,
don't know what yesterday I wrote or the date.
    Where, when the kettle hums, the wet fog's weft
    invites a stranger through a window's cleft,
    and thousands live wall-to-wall, lone forlorn men,
    in London I would like to be again.

SCHULSCHLUSS IN DER BÜCHEREI

Nun wird es stiller in der Bücherei;
nur manchmal, während ich mir nach der Reih
die Bände ordne und ins Fach sie rück,
kommt ein Student noch, bringt ein Buch zurück.

So manche haben hier mich gern gesehn,
die nun von hier hinaus ins Leben gehn.
Sie alle fanden bei mir Gastlichkeit,
gab ihnen mehr als nur von meiner Zeit,

empfahl manch Buch, das nicht im Lehrplan war.
Was wird aus ihnen werden übers Jahr?
Vielleicht, daß mir von ihnen einer schreibt,
wie's ihm ergeht. Ich aber bin, der bleibt

für sie, die kommen, der zu jeder Frist
hier wie ein Buch für sie zu finden ist,
worin man nachschlägt; und es wird von mir,
geh ich einst, etwas noch verweilen hier,

END OF TERM IN THE LIBRARY

Now that the library's rush has come and gone,
a kind of afterthought–while in my nook
I file loose volumes till each shelf is done!–
a student enters to return a book.

There are some who did like to see me here,
who hence now step to also join life's war.
To all of them I've lent a friendly ear,
and more than just the time I've served so far,

suggesting books not on their reading list . . .
What will now happen to them in a year?
Someone might write me of himself the gist.
But I'm the one who always will be here

for those who visit this place at any time,
like an odd book on our library's shelf
wherein to browse . . . and some things of mine
will stay here when long gone I myself.

ABSCHIED VON DER BÜCHEREI

Ich werde nicht mehr lang hier bleiben,
das macht mein Tagwerk nun so leer;
ich sehe der Studenten Treiben,
doch es betrifft mich schon nicht mehr.
Das Fachblatt wird noch durchgenommen,
ich räum die Bücher täglich ein;
doch wann, die ich bestelle, kommen,
wird Bücherwart ein andrer sein.

Ich werde nicht mehr lang hier bleiben;
viel auszustelln wär meine Pflicht,
doch sich mit der Kanzlei zu reiben
und zu verfeinden, lohnt sich nicht.
Ich bin nicht stets ganz da für jeden
und laß in kein Gespräch mich ein;
denn was wir auch vertraut noch reden,
kann nur ein Abschiednehmen sein.

Ich werde nicht mehr lang hier bleiben;
ich seh nicht auf dem Sims den Staub,
ich seh nur durch die Fensterscheiben,
wie sich vom Baume löst das Laub.
Es dünkt samt ihren langen Tischen
die Bücherei mich seltsam weit;
und nur aus ihr mich auzuwischen,
wie ich es vorhab, tut mir leid.

FAREWELL TO THE LIBRARY

I won't stay on much longer here,
to start my day's work makes me ill;
I watch the students sport their gear,
yet my involvement now's but nil.
The index I still copy from,
I daily use the filing cards;
but when the books I've ordered come,
then other librarians be their guards.

I won't stay on much longer here,
displaying books would be my job,
yet enmity with clerks I fear,
to fend them off strength me would rob.
Just lately I have not been there
for readers discussing their achieve-
ments, confidences though we share:
I'll end it all by taking my leave.

I won't stay on much longer here;
ignoring on the sill dust's grief
I look on trees through windows clear,
how foliage drops leaf by leaf.
Because the tables are so long
the library seems strangely wide;
erasing my own name from its throng
ahead of time–'es tut mir leid'!

120

PART VI

LOVE IN LONDON (1950-57)

NACH EINER NACHT IM HYDE PARK

Komm, laß uns tiefer in die Büsche rücken;
das erste Laub des Herbsts liegt weich zuhauf,
der Rasen ist besät mit steifen Mücken,
und durch die Bäume zieht der Tag herauf.
Vom Teich her wallt der Nebel kühl und fahl,
und dünn auf ihn legt sich der erste Strahl.

Laß dir die Halme aus den Haaren kämmen,
wie Milch steht weich der Flaum um dein Gesicht;
die leicht mir jäh die Augen überschwemmen,
der stillen Tränen achte, Molly, nicht.
Der Herbstrauch, der durchsonnt dir streift das Haar,
in meiner Heimat kocht den Wein er gar.

Schön ist das Land, aus dem sie mich vertrieben;
die Sterne der Zichorien blaun am Ranft,
blank sind die Quitten, die durchs Laub sich schieben,
und selbst der Rauch des Herbstes ist noch sanft.
Es sind die Stunden zwischen heiß und kalt
seit je des Landes sanfteste Gewalt.

O wär mir seine Leichtigkeit gegeben,
im Frösteln dich zu lieben, fremdes Kind,
und eine Spanne Zeit, in der mein Leben
in Liedern mohngleich aus der Kapsel rinnt,
es wär ein Dank für all die Freundlichkeit . . .
Es blinkt der Weg, es ist zu gehn schon Zeit.

AFTER A NIGHT IN HYDE PARK

Come, let's move deeper into the park's bushes,
where first leaves are quite softly heaped; the lawn
is covered over with stiff gnats, up pushes
through nearby trees a new day's bloody dawn.
Pale from the pond the fog rolls in on the glade,
and thin above the sun's first beam is laid.

The wind-blown grass-blades from your hair let's comb,
your face like milk is covered by soft fuzz;
if my eyes overflow hear I your groan,
ignore the tears, my darling Molly, for us.
The sun-bathed smoke of fall that streaks your hair
in my far homeland it ferments wine's air.

So nice the land from which I have been driven;
off the road blue endive stars, aloft
summer quince fruits yellow hue has given,
and even the autumnal mist is soft.
The hours of cold and hot I do endorse
always as my homeland's gentlest force.

If I only find the ease of being
I've lost, and love you shivering, foreign child,
and an extension of my life for freeing
songs like poppy seed from capsules wild;
it would to you my thanks be for your kindness . . .
Far traffic lights turn green, it's time to dress.

"THEODOR KRAMER LIEST
AUS NEUEN GEDICHTEN"

Drei Jahre hab ich nichts als nur geschrieben,
vor Menschen hab ich es erst jetzt getrieben;
mein Gott, wie ist das gestern schön gewesen,
ich könnte immer sitzen dort und lesen.

Ein Druck ist mir da von der Brust gefallen;
ich habe rein gemeint, ich müßte lallen,
so seltsam leicht ist alles mir gekommen . . .
die eigne Stimme hab ich feucht vernommen.

Und mehr hab ich getan als Toast geröstet;
vielleicht hab ich die Frau im Eck getröstet,
den Abgestumpften wieder Halt gegeben;
es steht sich wiederum dafür, zu leben.

Mein Gott, was kann ich alles mir verzeihen:
daß ich drauf aus bin, mir ein Pfund zu leihen,
daß ich umsonst bei jungen Freunden wohne,
daß ich noch zuzle an der neuen Krone.

Es hat ja doch einmal geschehen müssen;
zum herben Rotwein meines Lands und Nüssen
hat mich die Übersetzerin geladen:
sie weiß, was Balsaminen sind und Raden.

Drei Jahre hab ich nichts als nur geschrieben,
jetzt kann ich wieder alle Menschen lieben . . .
Mein Gott, es ist nicht ganz umsonst gewesen,
ich könnte immer sitzen dort und lesen.

AFTER A BLOOMSBURY HOUSE
POETRY READING

For three years I've done nothing else but writing;
just now on listeners I have set my sighting.
My God, how great it yesterday was, when *Lied*
after *Lied* forever I wanted there to read.

Then a pressure lifted from my chest;
I felt like babbling, like a baby caressed,
so strangely easy it was to shed all fear . . .
When moist-eyed my own voice I clearly did hear.

And more I've done–I feel–than making toast;
consoled a refugee woman mourning love's ghost,
gave many listless aliens back their drive;
it pays again for me to surrender to life.

My lord, my own sins now I can atone:
scheming to obtain a one-pound loan,
living rent-free with young friends in town,
sucking on my free new dental crown.

It just had to happen sometime–I knew in my guts!–
to be invited to red wine and nuts
by a translator friend at the best of hotels:
she knows what balsamines are and cockle shells.

For three years I've done nothing else but writing,
now I can love all people again without fighting . . .
My God, it wasn't all in vain that I fled,
I could have sat up front forever and read.

NUN DRUCKT MAN DRÜBEN WIEDER, WAS ICH SCHREIB . . .

Nun druckt man drüben wieder, was ich schreib;
es ist, als hätt ich einen zweiten Leib,
der wächst und breit in Positur sich stellt,
indes hier der, in dem ich haus, verfällt.

Er wächst und leidet kaum an etwas Not;
ich aber brauch's wie einen Bissen Brot,
daß jemand auf mich schaut die ganze Zeit,
und manchmal auch ein wenig Zärtlichkeit,

soll ich nicht schwinden, eh man sich's versieht.
Wer aber weiß schon, wie mir hier geschieht?
Und wer es weiß, der kümmert sich nicht drum;
es wächst mein Werk, doch meine Zeit ist um.

THEY REPRINT MY POEMS AGAIN
IN POSTWAR VIENNA

They reprint my poems now in postwar Vienna;
it's like I've suddenly got a twin-ghost penner
who's growing in stature in some surreal way,
while the real one here lives in decay.

He grows and hardly suffers hardships bad;
but I'm in need (an old chap looking sad!)
of someone now to look after me all the time,
and show some affection for a bloke like I'm,

or else I'll suddenly fade out, I fear.
But who then knows what to me happened here?
And those who know they simply couldn't care less;
my work collects–I'm soon passé, I guess.

LIEBE IN LONDON

Diesen heißen Sommer sind die Gassen
seltsam breit, so liegen sie verlassen,
und die Blätter fallen grün verdorrt;
wenn die Schoten schnellen, muß ich fort.

Nicht verlängert ward mein Paß, wir beide
sind hier, fremde Freundin, fremd . . . Wie Seide
schwebt's, da braucht es zwischen uns kein Wort;
wenn die Schoten schnellen, muß ich fort.

Können aber, drängt's uns, alles sagen,
können alles in den Nächten wagen,
gibt's doch, der uns aufnimmt, keinen Ort;
wenn die Schoten schnellen, muß ich fort.

LOVE IN LONDON

This hot summer streets look strangely wide;
that's how of all the traffic they're bereft,
and dried-out green leaves to earth down glide;
when the pods let fly, it's time I left.

My passport has run out; both legally dead,
strange love, we're aliens here . . . A silky weft
floats in the air, no word needs to be said;
when the pods let fly, it's time I left.

Though in despair we dare to tell each other
all, escaping into night's black cleft –
we know, for us no land's a father or mother;
when the pods let fly, it's time I left.

IM ANSTALTSGARTEN

Du sitzt im Garten vor dem Irrenhaus
scharf haucht dein Mund den gleichen Schlaftrunk aus;
bin auf Parole sieben Wochen nun:
ich möcht das Tier mit den zwei Rücken tun.

Was dich verstört hat, Mädel, frag ich nicht;
in deinen Augen glimmt ein grünes Licht:
das sehnt sich nicht nach Schminke nur und Schuhn,
das will das Tier mit den zwei Rücken tun.

Oh wär's zur Zeit der Morgenrunde Nacht,
wär's schwarz, geräuschlos auf der Stell gemacht,
wir könnten unterm süßen Flieder ruhn
und dort das Tier mit den zwei Rücken tun.

BROCKWOOD GARDENS

Early you sit on the lawn in front of the madhouse,
exhaling nightcap's bitter taste; I relax
for seven weeks on parole, my mind to delouse:
I like to do the beast with the two backs.

What had you upset, girl, I shan't ask;
in your green eyes there is a sparkle of sex
that yearns not just for pumps and makaeup flask,
but wants to do the beast with the two backs.

If you were a night-nurse on morning rounds,
we both then under lilac could relax,
after we had done, on hospital grounds,
the ancient game of the beast with the two backs.

DER RIVER WEY

Ein trüber Fluß, der nie im Lauf sich hetzt,
zuweilen schmal, oft seicht, von Schilf durchsetzt,
von Dorn und Disteln, dann von Gras und Klee
umstanden nur; das ist der River Wey.

Ich ging–mir war vor meiner Angst schon bang–
im Sommer oft ihn nachts den Pfad entlang;
zu schlammig schien–ich biß die Hand mir weh–
drin zu ertrinken, mir der River Wey.

Freiwillig war ich lang im Irrenhaus.
Die alte Brücke sieht heut seltsam aus;
und bin doch froh, daß ich dich wiederseh,
von fahlem Ried durchsetzt, mein River Wey.

THE RIVER WEY

A muddy stream that hardly ever speeds,
that's narrow at times, oft shallow, full of reeds,
on whose banks thorny thistles interlay
the grass and clover; that's the River Wey.

I've walked–the sense of my own fear quite strong!–
on summer nights quite oft its path along;
too muddy it seemed; my hand I bit sore while delay-
ing up to drown myself in the River Wey.

I committed myself voluntarily to the ward.
The old bridge does look strange today (*en garde!*);
yet when on you I cast my eyes each day
again I'm glad, my reed-covered River Wey.

PART VII

RETURN TO VIENNA (1957)

HEIMKEHR

Die Täler und Höhn sind die alten,
der Weiser spreizt plump an der Kehr
die Hand, doch die alten Gestalten,
ich such sie und find sie nicht mehr,
der Roßkamm, der Felljud, die Kunden,
die launig die Hohlwege ziehn,
sie sind aus dem Weinland geschwunden;
der Löß weht über sie hin.

Der Bettler kommt nicht aus dem Kotter
im März, kehrt nicht heim, löst sich fahl
das Laub, in die Zelle. Der Strotter
geht nicht mehr entlang am Kanal.
Er läßt nicht, gebückt, viele Stunden
nach Hadern den Krallenstock ziehn;
sie sind von den Stätten geschwunden;
der Schutt weht über sie hin.

Der Tippler läßt nicht statt mit Brühe
sich fülln mehr mit Hansel die Rein;
es kehrt nicht mehr schon in der Frühe
der Säufer beim Branntweiner ein.
Daheim wieder, euch zu bekunden
wie mich, ist mir Stimme verliehn;
ich singe und bin schon geschwunden;
der Staub weht über mich hin.

HOMECOMING

The hills and valleys are the old ones,
and crooked signposts still straddle roads' fork,
but the locals I knew from my youthful runs
I'd find them only at the morgue:
horse traders, pelt Jews, clients and friends
who the lanes with a song did travel,
they've vanished from the sloping winelands;
the wind the loess over them blows level.

The beggar from jail does no more decamp
as usual in March, to return when last leaves
fall, to his cell. The scavenger tramp
no more with his hook retrieves
the rags and tatters from Vienna's Canal
by walking for hours on end bent low;
they've faded from their hideouts all;
over them the trash winds blow.

The dipso who filled not with kitchen
soup but liquor his casserole,
he's stopped to feed his early itching
at the distiller's from his bowl.
Back home again, to you to prove
that I've indeed my voice regained,
I sing – as tourists say – in the groove;
in the blowing dust I am engrained

WIEDERSEHEN MIT DER HEIMAT

Nach Jahren kam, verstört, ich wieder her;
der alten Gassen manche sind nicht mehr,
der Ringturm kantig sich zum Himmel stemmt:
erst in der Heimat bin ich ewig fremd.

Mir schließt sich im Gedächtnis nicht das Loch;
Espressos glitzern, mich empfängt kein Tschoch,
das Moped braust, nur hastig wird geschlemmt:
erst in der Heimat bin ich ewig fremd.

Sind auch die Lüfte anderswo bewohnt,
mir ist, als zielte alles nach dem Mond,
der saugte, zwischen Dächern eingeklemmt:
erst in den Heimat bin ich ewig fremd.

HOMETOWN REVISITED

After years, bewildered, I'm back by air,
some inner city streets can find no longer there.
Sharply the Ring Tower to the sky does prod:
only at home I feel I am forever abroad.

Canal-bench memories I cannot put away.
Espressos glitter; closed though is my old café
Mopeds roar, while lunch in passing but is caught:
only at home I feel I am forever abroad

Elsewhere-like Paris, for instance:-people say: *la lune*.
I think these days the whole world's aiming for the moon
that sucks me up, hemmed in by slanting rooftops odd:
only at home I feel I am forever abroad.

EPILOGUE

DER GROSSE BRUDER

Vergangen sind nun an die fünfzig Jahr,
doch immer ist's noch, wie es früher war.

Der große Bruder bin ich, er ist klein,
und nichts, so scheint's, kann dran gerüttelt sein.

Er kommt zu mir, bedrängt ihn was, und flennt,
und ob auch heut der Ozean uns trennt.

Ein Unternehmen hab ich, Frau und Geld,
er siecht im Dienst, doch schreibt, was ihm gefällt.

Ob's taugt, ob nicht, ist nicht für mich der Kern:
ich mag ihn nicht und hab ihn dennoch gern.

MY BIG BROTHER IN AMERICA

Though after fifty years we are grayed men,
things are the same with us, as they were then.

I'm big brother, that's me, and he's the kid,
and nothing at all, it seems, can be done about it.

To me he comes in distress, on my shoulder to cry,
though we today the big lake must defy.

A thriving business I got, a family and funds,
he's ailing and hates his job, but writes what he wants,

doesn't matter to me if it sells or remains *anonym:*
I don't like him much, and yet I'm fond of him.

AFTERWORD

In the night of April 28-29, 1992, a personal tragedy unfolded in New York City, a town aplenty with human disasters on any given day, where 'minor' fatalities attract no attention at all in the media.[1] Following a specially arranged two-day working session with his editor-friend Jörg Thunecke to finalize a three-year translation project of selected exile poems by the Austrian writer Theodor Kramer (1897-1958), the poet-translator and fellow emigré Frederick (Fritz) Brainin (*1913) was taken ill in the Lower Manhattan studio of Kramer's niece Edith, and, by a bizarre coincidence, died in his apartment in Queens while his younger collaborator was watching the black comedy *Passed Away* in a cinema on 13th Street.

Brainin's untimely death marked the sad end of a friendship between artist and academic–the latter being left with the responsibility for the unfinished product–which had begun some three years earlier in 1990, when the author of this "Afterword" and collaborator in the verse translations of Kramer's poems published for the first time in this volume, visited Brainin in his 18th floor abode in Flushing overlooking La Guardia Airport and persuaded him to revisit his hometown Vienna after an absence of fifty years.

Brainin, born on 22 August 1913 in Vienna's Second District, was the son of a sculptor-father of Lithuanian-Jewish origin. Young Brainin spent the 1920s as a pupil in a Vienna grammar school whence he graduated in 1931. While still in school he came under the influence of Dr. Viktor Frankl and the publisher Erwin von Barth-Wehrenalp who encouraged him to start writing poetry. The first result of such efforts was a slim volume of poems entitled *Alltag, Gedichte 1926-1929,* in addition to numerous publications in Viennese literary journals and newspapers, above all the

Wiener Arbeiter-Zeitung, poems which have since been collected and published by Eckart Früh.[2] A few years after the *Arbeiter-Zeitung* ceased publication in 1934, Brainin managed to get yet another volume of poems published *Die eherne Lyra* (1936); however, following the annexation of Austria by the Nazis in March 1938 the position of left-wing writers and Jews like Brainin became untenable, and he emigrated to the United States, where he arrived in October 1938.

In the wake of his forced departure from Austria, Brainin found it initially quite hard to adjust to the new way of life in the country which had offered him refuge. Between 1939 and 1942 he worked in various low-paying jobs while trying to stay in touch with his native country. In 1943, though, when drafted into the United States army, and eventually assigned to the U.S. Secret Service to work in German and Austrian POW camps in the Midwest, an experience which led to severe psychic disorders and his eventual discharge from active military service, this attitude changed and made him address himself increasingly to the American way of life.

In 1949 Brainin married Florence Priluc and set up house in New York City, first in Upper Manhattan, later in Brooklyn, and eventually in the Bronx, before assuming his final quarters in Queens. In 1950 a son, Perry Isak, was born, and Brainin led a quiet, withdrawn life, working as a free-lance translator and writing poetry in his spare time, until in the 1980s two tragic events overshadowed, and permanently changed, his existence: the murder of his son, leading to the subsequent mental illness of his wife, who also died in the middle of that decade.

In the autumn of 1988, at the invitation of the Viennese "Kunstverein," and with the active support of Viennese writer and academic Dr. Konstantin Kaiser, who rediscovered the poet in the mid-1980s, Brainin finally did revisit the town of his birth for the first time in fifty years, as suggested to him by Jörg Thunecke during his visit in the spring of that year. This was followed by a second visit in spring 1990 on the occasion of the publication of his collection of poems entitled *Das siebte Wien*.[3] Brainin, who prior to 1938 had been thought of as one of Austria's lyric hopefuls, never ceased writing poetry during his years in exile, notwithstanding the fact that for a couple of decades–the 1950s and 1960s–he was presumed missing in German-speaking lands. His poetic diction, though, had changed irreversibly as the result of his exposure to urban American, particularly New York, society and its environment, and he gradually began to abandon German as his literary medium, adopting American-English as the vehicle for his poetic work.[4] Which is to say that there are signs of an increasing number of poems written in English since the 1950s, as well as growing evidence of Americanisms in his remaining German work, to a point where such poems became a kind of admix of English and German, whichever word or expression in either language best suited the given poetic situation. At the same time though, while this kind of linguistic mixture often led to questionable aesthetic results in Brainin's own poetic products, it seems to have predestined him to become one of America's best translators of urban poetry, a point which was not lost on the author of this Afterword when looking for someone to translate Theodor Kramer's exile poems of urban English life in the 1940s and 1950s.[5] As a result it was agreed during Brainin's second stay in Vienna that he should be commissioned to provide verse translations of about fifty Kramer poems of his own choice, written by the latter in exile in England, reviving earlier plans between Kramer and Brainin dating back to 1948.[6] Jörg Thunecke was to act as reader, advising Brainin on English ways of life, on local color, geographical and historical details as pertaining to Kramer's country of refuge, while at the same time smoothing out– though *not* in a censorial capacity–some of the extremes of Brainin's urban New York diction, in an attempt to make the translations intelligible also to an English-speaking audience outside the United States.

*

Theodor Kramer, the poet who died in Vienna on 14 April 1958 shortly after returning to his native Austria following an eighteen-year absence in England, was the son of a Jewish country physician, born in Lower Austria on New Year's Day 1897. From the very beginning two formative experiences vitally and permanently influenced his poetic diction as well as his choice of subject, affecting his whole oeuvre; the economic crisis and hardship of the 1920s and 1930s in Austria, and the local landscape and people of the part of Austria (Niederösterreich and Burgenland) he was born into and which he traveled extensively as a young man. Kramer was drafted into the Austro-Hungarian army during World War One, but was discharged in 1916 following a serious facial injury. He subsequently enrolled at the University of Vienna but found it difficult to support himself during the years of economic recession, quit being a student, and trained to become a book dealer.

His first literary breakthrough came in 1929, when the German publishers Rütten & Loening accepted his *Gaunerzinke,* a slim volume of lyric poems signaling a departure from well-worn paths of traditional poetry, being part of a new literary movement labeled "Neue Sachlichkeit" (new matter-of-factness), emphasizing the harshness of local environment and attaching great importance to the immediacy of images conveyed, a movement which marked the beginning of Kramer's fame as a poet, and which is also typical for quite a few of his poems written later in the United Kingdom. Kramer subsequently succeeded in publishing a number of follow-up volumes in the 1930s: *Kalendarium* (1930), another collection of early poetry, and most importantly a volume of war poems entitled *Wir lagen in Wolhynien im Morast* (1931), which–as far as poetry goes–compares favorably with Remarque's famous anti-war novel *All Quiet on the Western Front* (1929), and eventually the collection *Mit der Ziehharmonika* (1936).[7] However, following the attack on Austria's democratic institutions in the aftermath of the abortive February 1934 uprising which led to the establishment of a crypto-Fascist state, the so-called "Ständestaat," Kramer, like Brainin and many other writers on the left of the political spectrum, was deprived of his regular literary outlets and experienced a severe decline in income, a process which climaxed after the Anschluss of Austria to the German Reich in March 1938, leading to his emigration to England in February 1939.[8]

During his years of exile in Britain, including the postwar period, Kramer never stopped writing poetry in German, producing literally thousands of poems, mirroring, among other topics, life in Vienna during the harrowing months immediately following the Nazi takeover, his initial stay in London, the traumatic experience of internment on the Isle of Man during the second half of 1940, his release in January 1941 and subsequent life in the so-called Black Country area in the British Midlands, with its bleak industrial landscape, highly reminiscent of parts of his native Austria. In addition he describes his move to Guildford in southern England as a librarian at the beginning of 1943, not to mention the countless trials and tribulations, hopes and fears of exile existence with its manifold cultural, linguistic and personal problems, leading to his eventual return to Austria, a forgotten and forlorn figure, shortly

149

before his early death in 1958.[9]

Theodor Kramer's unique contribution to lyric poetry of the late 1920s and 1930s, which he continued in exile in Britain throughout the 1940s and 1950s, was the creation of a so-called "Ästhetik des Besonderen," a special kind of aesthetics typified by its highly regionalistic vocabulary, and categorized by labels like "Heimatkunst" (regional or provincial art) and "Neue Sachlichkeit."[10] His poetic diction, characterized by an obsession for concentrating on specific details about people at the bottom end of the social scale, their lives and their environment, focuses heavily on nouns, employing a highly esoteric kind of terminology, which nowadays requires outsiders to resort to Austrian dialect dictionaries, or to consult word lists appended to publications of his poetry! In other words, Kramer homed in on descriptive details of once-popular, typical jobs and livelihoods, of people at the very edge of society, providing a vivid account of their perilous daily existence, interlacing it with a wide range of images drawn from the Austrian landscape and local color, and from everyday objects (so-called "Alltagsdinge") and items like tools, irretrievably lost today, typical for crafts and trades of a bygone era of Austria's past. Three criteria thus tend to dominate Kramer's poetic work: the local color of Lower Austria; the simplicity of the rhyme patterns; and the concentration on themes and motifs about the milieu of society's poorest and its outcasts.

Bearing in mind, therefore, the exclusivity and repetitiveness of Kramer's use of a certain unique range of stylistic features in his poetry in the 1930s, steeped as they were in regionalistic aspects of a remote part of prewar Austria, it may come as a bit of a surprise to readers of Kramer's exile poetry that he did not try harder to supplant key elements of his poetic diction with similar aspects of rural

150

and/or industrial life in England, that the so-called "Umin-strumentierung" (Chvojka) of experiences in his native Austria to those of the country of refuge did not take place to a far larger extent. This Afterword cannot be the place to look for explanations for this peculiar phenomenon; yet it should be mentioned, at least in passing, that, with the encouragement of Jörg Thunecke, Brainin in his selection of poetry written by Kramer in exile, focused specifically on the limited number of poems which do allow the reader to draw parallels with similar poems by the same author written in the 1930s against an Austrian background.

Kramer's life had been blighted long before the annexation of Austria in March 1938, for the rise of the Nazis in power in early 1933 and the establishment of Austro-Fascism in 1934, severely hampered his literary work by restricting outlets in German-speaking areas, a situation aggravated by the events of November 1938 ("Reichskristallnacht"), which led to a life of constant fear of persecution and/or arrest until his eventual emigration to Britain in 1939. In an effort to recreate the horrors of life in Vienna for Jews in the aftermath of Anschluss and "Kristallnacht," a small number of poems have been included in this volume to mirror these months as experienced by Kramer himself, inasmuch as quite a number of the relatively few poems reflecting the actual exile situation in England shortly after Kramer's arrival in London in late 1939 have also been chosen; they highlight his mood (characterized by intense self-observation and emphasis on his personal sufferings at times amounting to self-pity) during these first few months prior to internment in mid-1940; his problems with the English language and the daily habits of his British hosts; his pecuniary problems, as much as his constant loneliness, echoed in his laments about a lack of personal contacts in his new environment; the shock of internment in

151

May 1940 in a camp on the relatively remote Isle of Man in the Irish Sea, soon superseded by his bitterness toward his British hosts over their treatment of refugees in the United Kingdom. After his release in early January 1941 Kramer lived for just under two years in the West Midlands, an area in many ways akin to his native Lower Austria, and a number of the poems chosen for this publication (from "Slums and Black Country," written 1944-1947), are based on the description of the natural and industrial landscape of the so-called Black Country district near Birmingham, at that time the site of the largest iron and steel industry in Britain. As in his earlier poetry about regional parts of Austria during the inter-war years, Kramer's diction in his poems about the English Midlands, written in the 1940s, abounds with typical aspects of everyday life and local color, despite the fact that a considerable weakening of his creative imagination seems to have occurred, noticeable, above all, in the lack of linguistic integration of the specific terminology at one time used to characterize this part of England, and notwithstanding the fact that Kramer, in all his years in exile, never responded as positively to, and never felt as much at home in, any other part of England. Many of the English loan words, in otherwise wholly German texts, constitute a decidedly weak feature, and are indicative of the aesthetic crisis Kramer was experiencing during his years in England. Their use shows that he was unable to adjust fully to changing conditions, that he failed to join negative reality and positive imagination as in his highly accomplished poems of the 1930s, and that he too often indulged in nostalgic reflections of the past rather than adapt to new circumstances. Brainin, who no doubt experienced similar problems during his early years in exile in New York, managed, above everything else in his translations, to capture beautifully the spirit of these poems and get their message across to prospective readers in a kind of American-English which, hopefully, will enable them to put themselves into the mind of a poet at odds with his surroundings (echoed by a long list of negative points about his host country), while at the same time pining for his native country Austria, and writing vastly more poems about it than about England, yet refusing to return home for years after the end of the war.

Closely linked to Kramer's attempted aesthetic adaptation of his erstwhile German diction to the needs of his poems about Black Country industrial landscapes, city slums and working-class people are certain social aspects; for Kramer was not merely appalled by the devastation wrought by heavy industry in this Midland region, he was even more interested in details of the social infrastructure of the area, that is, keen about the picture of a society tied, for better or for worse, to its surrounding countryside and industry. Quite a few of the poems chosen by Brainin therefore also herald Kramer's return to social criticism after a break of some ten years, giving vent to his reawakened social conscience and his compassion with the sufferings of the underprivileged masses of the population. Although in most cases the end product of his lyric efforts was not exactly high-class poetry, Kramer's extraordinary gift for precise observation, particularly the details of the flaws in industrial English society, make these poems unique historical documents of a bygone era in British history. Consequently, Frederick Brainin is to be given credit, posthumously, for having made a selection of very typical poems and for rendering them accessible to a wider English-speaking audience whose past everyday life they so vividly portray.

Notes

1. For details see Jörg Thunecke's obituary: "Frederick Brainin–Dichter und Übersetzer," in: *Mit der Ziehharmonika. Zeitschrift der Theodor Kramer Gesellschaft* (Vienna) 9 (December 1992), 4, pp. 2-17.

2. Kurt Faecher (= Eckhart Früh). *Noch mehr. Fritz Brainin–Gedichte* (Vienna, 1984). Kurt Faecher, *Noch mehr. Städtische Landschaftsstudien und andere Gedichte von Fritz Brainin* (Vienna, 1988). Kurt Faecher, *Noch mehr. Fritz Brainin–Ozeanflieger* (Vienna, 1992).

3. Cf. Jörg Thunecke's "Nachwort" to *Das siebte Wien* (Vienna: Verlag für Gesellschaftskritik, 1990), pp. 137-146.

4. Cf. Jörg Thunecke's Brainin-Bibliography in John Spalek, Hrsg., *Guide to Archival Materials of the German-Speaking Emigration to the United States after 1933*, Vol. 2 (Munich: Saur Verlag, 1994) (forthcoming).

5. Cf. "Der junge Kramer–The Young Kramer. Acht Nachdichtungen von Fritz Brainin," in: *Mit der Ziehharmonika, 10 (1993)*, 1, pp. 9-12. Cf. also Jörg Thunecke, "Kästner-Übertragungen von Frederick Brainin," in: *Mit der Ziehharmonika, 10 (1993)*, 3, pp. 6-7.

6. Cf. three letters by Kramer to Brainin, dating back to late 1948, while the latter was still in a New York veterans' hospital (the full text of these letters will be published in *Mit der Ziehharmonika* 11 [1994], 2 [forthcoming]; all translations are Brainin's and have been adopted without alterations). In his letter of 11 November 1948, Kramer complains about the poor quality of the translation of one of his poems ("Hitler over Vienna," published without authorization, in *War Poems of the United Nations*, edited by Joy Davidman [New York, 1943], pp. 11-14]: "My English is very poor, but adequate to judge that the translation is out for sensation, and a very poor one," Kramer wrote in the follow-up letter of 18 November 1948. Kramer responds to a proposal by Brainin in his letter of 13 November 1948 (which must be presumed lost, like all his other letters to Kramer): "I'm sure your translator's style would differ from that practiced in that splendid anthology I've mentioned. But before I send you something, I like to stipulate two conditions, and I don't know whether or not you'll accept them. The first is that I must approve a translation or adaptation prior to its publication by you. The second is that nothing by me may be published free of charge. In this connection I got my own strict guidelines, and I've held also in England the emigrant press to it, and only in the case of the

Austro-American Tribune I've forgotten to settle this matter. I would suggest to split any fee on a fifty-fifty basis, because aside from your translator's labor you would have the trouble of getting anything into print. But this key, of course, is quite important."

The matter was raised once more in the third, and seemingly final, letter of Kramer's to Brainin during this period (of 30 December 1948), when Kramer informed Brainin: "From Guildford . . . I'll send my two small volumes as soon as I get them from Vienna, and maybe a few manuscripts. Any fee I expect you to share with me, that's customary, because of your labor involved. Without any fee payable to me I don't want to publish, I got my principles there. But you haven't written me yet whether I can see the translation in advance, and any publication thereof depends on my agreement. I really hope that you don't take this as an offence, I would do this always, without exception."

After this the correspondence between Brainin and Kramer apparently ended, and the translation project never got off the ground. Despite this, Brainin seems to have nourished the idea of translating select poems by Kramer into English. In connection with this see the first verse of the German version of "The Displaced Poet" (in *Zehn Takte Weltmusik. Eine Lyrik-Anthologie des PEN-Zentrums deutschsprachiger Autoren im Ausland,* edited by Arno Reinfrank [Gerlingen: Bleicher Verlag, 1988], p. 49) entitled "Selbstbildnis als Übersetzer" (in *Das siebte Wien* (Vienna: Verlag für Gesellschaftskritik, 1990), p. 109: "Mein Traum war immer nur in einem billigen Quartier / zu leben–ein frührer Speicher laderampenventiliert?– / auf ein besonntes Gasserl hinaus beim Westside River-Pier, / wo Theodor Kramers Vers ich übersetz [in the original it was Brecht's verse] wenn ich stier / und wenn mein eigner Reim von Redakteurn wird retourniert."

7. Cf. Daniela Stigl, *"Wo niemand zuhaus ist, dort bin ich zuhaus." Theodor Kramer–Heimatdichter und Sozialdemokrat zwischen den Fronten* (Vienna: Böhlau Verlag, 1993).

8. Cf. Erwin Chvojka's "Einleitung" to *Theodor Kramer–Gesammelte Gedichte* 1 (Vienna, 1984), pp. 7–22.

9. Cf. the following selection of Kramer publications listed by Erwin Chvojka in *Orgel aus Staub* (Vienna/Zurich: Europa Verlag, 1991), p. 176; *Die Gaunerzinke* (1929); *Kalendarium* (1930); *Wir lagen in Wolkynien im Morast* (1931); *Mit der Ziehharmonika* (1936); *Verbannt aus Österreich* (1943); *Wien 1938–Die grünen Kader* (1946); *Die untere Schenke* (1946); *Vom schwarzen Wein* (1956); *Einer bezeugt*

es (1960); *Lob der Verzweiflung* (1972); *Lied am Rand* (1975); *Orgel aus Staub* (1983; rev. ed. 1991); *Gesammelte Gedichte*, 3 vols. (1984-1987).

10. Cf. Jörg Thunecke, "Zu Theodor Kramers Exillyrik. Versuch einer Ästhetik des Besonderen im nachgelassenen England-Buch," in: *Zwischenwelt. Jahrbuch der Theodor Kramer Gesellschaft* 1 (Vienna, 1990), pp. 165-198.

SOURCES AND DATES OF COMPOSITION

THE OLD ACCORDIONIST

Nicht fürs Süße, nur fürs Scharfe . . .
(30.1.1952; E: Büg 4/52; Q: GG 3/640)

I THE LAST DAYS IN VIENNA (1938)

An eine junge Freundin
(7.7.1932; E: AZ 20.6.1933; Q:GG 1/202)

Die Wahrheit ist, man hat mir nichts getan
(13.7.1938; TA; Q: GG 1/352)
An mein Kaffeehaus
(6.5.1938; Q: GG 1/351)
Von der Angst
(21.7.1938; Q: GG 1/354)
Wer läutet draußen an der Tür?
(18.6.1938; 2.Druckfassung; Q: GG 1/355)
Wien, Fronleichnam 1939
(6.10.1941; 1.Druckfassung; Q: GG 1/300)
Das Konsulat
(9.7.1953; E: Aufb 30.4.1954; Q: GG 2/137)

II THIS ISLAND CALLED HOME (1939)

Von dem ersten Tagen in London
(12.8.1942; Q: GG 2/138)
Hanover Square
(17.5.1945; Q: GG 2/155)
Zuhaus in London
(3.1.1956; Q: GG 3/678)
Das Blechdach
(23.12.1955; Q: GG 3/678)
Der kleine Square
(26.8.1944; Q: GG 2/207)
Fremd in London
(12.8.1942; Q: GG 2/181)

Das Telephon
(20.5.1953; Q: GG 2/190)
Verlassenheit, Verlassenheit . . .
(6.7.1946; Q: GG 2/190-91)
Im Hochhaus
(27.8.1946; Q: GG 2/205)
In einer Untergrundbahnstation
(10.12.1941; Q: GG 1/107)
Auf ein grünes Trümmerfeld
(1.8.1944; Q: GG 2/204)
Fremd für immer
(9.12.1941; Q: GG 2/151)
Es mögen andre eine Heimat suchen . . .
(28.9.1941); Q: GG 2/185)
Alte Freunde
(3.5.1944; Q: GG 2/194)

III ISLE OF MAN (1940-41)

Auf der Lore
(27.9.1940; Q: GG 2/156)
Die Internierten von Huyton
(23.5./23.6.1940); Q: 2/160-61)
Nach der Zuweisung des Zimmers
(11.9.1940; Q: GG 2/157)
So lieg ich ein zwei Stunden . . .
(5.9.1940; Q: GG 2/159)
Das Haferfeld
(28.8.1940; Q: GG 2/168)
Über den Stacheldraht
(31.8.1940; Q: GG 2/162)
Ich bin von Früh bis Abend müd . . .
(29.8.1940; Q: GG 2/158)
Drei grüne Bäume
(21.9.1940; Q: GG 2/167-68)
Und der Abend ist lang . . .
(18.10.1940; Q: GG 2/169)
An meine Mutter
(11.10.1940; Q: GG 2/178-79)

Was soll ich dir denn schreiben
(3.9.1940; Q: 1/294-95)
Lied für Verbannte
(18.5.1942; Q: GG 1/322)
Wir haben nicht Zeit
(20.10.1942; Q: GG 1/316)
Lied der Deportierten
(26.8.1940; Q: GG 2/170-71)
Entlassung
(20.10.1940; Q: GG 2/180)

IV SLUMS AND BLACK COUNTRY (1942-43)

Black Country
(28.5.1944; Q: GG 2/228)
Lob des Pubs
(5.6.1947; E: GTCM Sommer 49; Q: GG 2/246)
Fish and Chips
(4.4.1944; Q: GG 2/244)
Auf einen Vogelbeerbaum in Staffordshire
(14.22.9.1941; Q: GG 1/291-92)
Die Downs
(4.6.1947; Q: GG 2/250)

V GUILDFORD CAMPUS (1944-49)

Heimweh nach London
(18./29.6.1943; Q: GG 2/210)
Schulschluß in der Bücherei
(23.7.1947; Q: GG 2/211)
Abschied von der Bücherei
(15.6.1946; Q: GG 2/218)

VI LOVE IN LONDON (1950-57)

Nach einer Nacht im Hyde Park
(13.9.1942; E: AGM 42; Q: GG 2/199)
"Theodor Kramer liest aus neuen Gedichten"

(3.8.1942; Q: GG 2/214)
Nun druckt man drüben wieder, was ich schreibe
(3.9.1947; Q: GG 2/223)
Liebe in London
(23.4.1957; Q: GG 2/219)
Im Anstaltsgarten
(5.8.195; Q: GG 3/576)
Der River Wey
(7.12.1954; Q: GG 3/578)
Heimkehr
(17.3.1946; E: ÖT 25.5.46; Q: GG 2/271)
Wiedersehen mit der Heimat
(28.11.1957; Q: GG 3/590)
Der große Bruder
(18.2.1954; E: WH 12.11.54; Q: OaS 164)

VII RETURN TO VIENNA (1957)

Heimkehr
(17.3.1946; E: ÖT 25.5.46; Q: GG 2/221)
Wiedersehen mit der Heimat
(28.11.1957; Q: GG 3/590)

EPILOGUE

Der große Bruder
(18.2.1954; E: WH 12.11.54; Q: OaS 164)

ABBREVIATIONS

E (Erstdruck) = First Printed Version
Q (Quelle) = Source
TA (Titel/Anfangszeile) = Title/First Line
Druckfassung = Printed Version
Auf = Der Aufbau (New Work)
Büg = Die Büchergilde (Vienna)
GG = Theodor Kramer: Gesammelte Gedichte I-III, ed., Erwin Chvojka
     (Vienna: Europaverlag, 1984, 1985, 1987)

GTCM = Guildford Technical College Magazine
OaS = Theodor Kramer: Orgel aus Staub. Gedichte, ed. Erwin Chvojka
(Vienna: Europaverlag, ^{2}1991)
ÖT = Österreichisches Tagebuch (Vienna)
WA = Welt der Arbeit (Cologne)
ZGM = Zwischen gestern und morgen. Anthologie, ed. by Austrian
Centre Young Austria (London: 1942)

ARIADNE PRESS
Translations Series

ARIADNE PRESS
Translation Series